MAKING CHURCH MARKETING SIMPLE

The 6 Questions Every
Church Leader Needs to Answer

MADISEN K. MAYFIELD

Cover Design and Book Formatting by Madisen K. Mayfield

DEDICATION

To my parents and brother

To Chestnut Mountain Church

To the church marketers, communicators, and creatives of the world

This book is for you.

—BONUS—

After reading this book, the greatest thing that you can do is to put everything you learned into action.

That's why I'm giving you my
Making Church Marketing Simple Question Guide
for FREE!

DOWNLOAD THIS GUIDE FOR FREE NOW:
www.madisenmayfield.com/mcms

CONTENTS

PREFACE

"What are you doing for Me?"

I kept hearing this question in my head while the congregation was singing the hymn on that particular Sunday morning in 2012. No matter how much louder I kept singing trying to avoid this silent voice, it felt like the question kept getting louder and louder in my head until it was all I could hear, and I couldn't avoid it any longer. Enough was enough. I had an answer, "I'm doing everything I can for You. I go to youth group every Sunday, every Wednesday, I serve in the children's ministry. I'm only 15 years old. Why can't You call that person over in that pew?"

Side Note: Learn a lesson from me to never question God like this and try to tell Him what He should do instead.

After that answer, I put the question I had heard in the back of my head, tried to forget about it, and carried on with my high school life. The question came haunting back in the early spring semester of my 10th grade year when I was told that I would have to participate in an internship for my junior and senior year. This was my chance to finally break away from the graphic design, the print design, the web design, and the marketing opportunities that had followed me by 'accident' since my 13-year-old self was thrown an Adobe Photoshop book just for fun. This was my chance to finally pursue that medical career I wanted. As I heard the words, 'have to participate in an internship,' there was that question again, "What are you doing for Me?" As I filled out my internship application, the question kept getting louder and louder until, again, enough was enough. I finally decided to ask God what this question meant. That's when it all changed for me. Over the next several days, I began to see every graphic design, print design, web design, and marketing opportunity that my school had given me in a different perspective. What if these opportunities were not distractions, but instead they were talent builders? Then, three words popped into my head: "MARKETING THE MINISTRY". I redid my entire internship application and sat down in my school program interview to confidently say I wanted to intern at a church in the areas of graphic design and marketing and my end-of-year project for this entire internship would be called "Marketing the Ministry". When the panel asked me why? I responded with this entire story you have been reading. As I walked out of that interview, I hoped that I had not blown it because I ran that interview like I had already been accepted. A few weeks later I got the acceptance letter, leaving me feeling happy to have been accepted but also overwhelmed because I knew I would actually have to dive into the church marketing world now.

As the next school year approached, I was excited to get started and was even going to intern at the church my family was a part of at the time. God allowed to get my bearings for about three months until, in a whirlwind manner, I found myself as an intern at a larger local church. It was the same church where my parents were married. The same church where the freelance graphic designer's contract was expiring. The same church where on the first day they looked at my young, naive, 16-year-old self and said, "You're the graphic designer and these are all the platforms we have to display graphics on." This only added to the overwhelm!

I had to believe that God was getting quite a laugh at this because I was literally spinning as to how I would fake it until I made it. I was still a student. I was only sixteen. I could not draw to save my life, unless you like good stick figure people. I was in no way a Photoshop or Illustrator master. But there was no way around it. This church needed someone to be their graphic designer, and I was determined to learn how to do it well.

Almost seven years have passed since stepping into the church marketing world as an intern. I finished my internship there (eventually becoming the Director of Marketing and Communications there too after my undergrad); graduated high school, earned a Digital Marketing and Advertising degree; work with other churches, non-profits, and small businesses with their branding, graphic design, communications, and marketing; earned my Master's in Strategic Communication; and wrote this book. Working with churches of all sizes and being a part of churches of all sizes, I have been able to see many perspectives of how churches both reach and fail to reach people. Churches that do marketing well and churches that think marketing is only for big corporations. In my first-hand experience, I have seen how desperately churches need to communicate the Good News of Jesus Christ to this lost and dying world that surrounds us. Knowing this has led me to write this book. I want to help those of you who are just like me, the church marketers of the world.

CHAPTER 1
INTRODUCTION

If you've picked up this book, you are probably one of the following people: a pastor or secretary who wears many hats, a volunteer who wants to do more in their church and help bring it into the 21st Century, or even a church staff member who has been hired for church marketing.

However, no matter what category of people you fall under, there are four things that you and I have in common:
1. a love for Jesus
2. a love for His Church
3. a passion to serve the local church and use your talents
4. a passion for seeing others come to know Jesus and come to church.

These loves, passions, interests, and talents have brought you to where you are today, diving into the marketing world in a church setting.

Whatever your position or title may be, at some point you have more than likely felt overwhelmed. That's why I have written this book: for you, the overwhelmed church marketer. I understand the different positions of this role: the social media person to the website person, to the bulletin person, to the sound person, to the IT person, to the graphic designer, to the first time guest gift-wrapper (and maybe after all of that you still have to preach on Sundays). Church marketers have a lot on their plates.

I get it, you are overwhelmed. How do I know this? Because I have been in your shoes.

Let me be clear: God will equip the called. It does not matter if you are self-taught or professionally trained or, like me, both. What matters is your willingness. Are you willing to learn? Are you willing to get better? What is the level of your willingness? Are you willing for God to equip an ordinary you to do His extraordinary work? To be honest, I have quit writing this book multiple times. I did not feel equipped or worthy to write this book for you. How could I know how to write a church marketing book when I am in the weeds of it all right now? Despite my uncertainty, I persisted with writing this book because I am willing to overcome to help you realize and understand how church marketing can be made simple. You reading this book shows me your willingness already. You taking the time to read this book shows your willingness to hone your skills, to get better, and to learn more.

The first sermon series I ever designed was called Miracle Man, which talked about how Jesus is the Miracle Man. I found it ironic because it would be a miracle if I could complete a decent sermon series without getting fired. During my Thanksgiving break just two weeks after being told about this sermon series design, I got to work designing options for artwork. I sat dazed in front of my computer for literal hours on end, staring at a blank Photoshop canvas on my screen. With the week winding down and Monday approaching, my time was closing in and I still had nothing for a design. I remember my mom coming into my room and seeing me continuing to stare into my computer. Seeing that I was stuck, she told me to take a break. Hours passed before I went back to my computer, but when I did, I opened my Bible first. With that Bible clutched in my hand, I broke. Being overwhelmed was drowning me and I had not even finished my first design. I began to fervently pray that God would somehow show me what I needed to focus the artwork on. How was I supposed to encompass the Miracle Man in one graphic?

Upon opening my Bible and reading Jesus' miracles on Earth and searching the verses to spark inspiration for that first design, I chose to focus on visualizing Jesus turning water into wine. We read about the account of Jesus' turning water into wine in John 2, and we see that Mary, His own mother, had faith in Jesus that He could fix the problem of having no wine and she told the servants to listen to whatever He said to do. Without hesitation, the servants immediately cast their faith in Jesus not knowing who He was and obeyed Him. It seemed ludicrous for those servants to do what Jesus told them to do, but nevertheless they did. That is the power of willingness.

Sometimes it may seem ridiculous that God has placed you where He has you to be involved in church marketing. God is the King of kings and the Lord of lords; He is constantly revealing Himself. Surely, the King of kings does not need us to promote Himself, right? However, I encourage you to see today, right where you are, that God has called you to this. The talents, skills, vision, and the tasks that lay ahead of you may all feel overwhelming. I truly believe that you have to have a deep love for God and His Church to walk in this role whatever it may look like to you.

Exercise: Pause. Think about the wedding at Cana. Can you inspire in yourself the same faith and trust in Jesus that the servants at the wedding had? I encourage you to lean to that faith and trust. Remember: you have been called to this.

Before we go any further, I want you to think about why you do what you do. Take a moment to answer these questions, whether you say it in your head or (even better) write the answers down to keep with you and guide you on this journey.

1. How did God lead you to this point?

2. Why do you care about telling the story of your church?

3. Why do you care about building your church's social media presence?

4. Why are you ensuring that your church has eye-catching sermon series artwork?

5. Why do you care that your church's website uses the latest trends?

6. Why do you care that your church has a smooth live stream broadcast every Sunday?

7. Why do you care that a church event be promoted?

While this is only the introduction, hear this: If you are feeling overwhelmed, it is distracting you from your purpose. The sense of overwhelm obstructs the view of your 'why'. The sense of overwhelm distracts you from doing the greater work that God has called you to. It may be weird and odd to think of marketing as a ministry. How could something that is studied and applied in businesses be applicable in church? Marketing is not small groups, or children's ministry, student ministry, or a mission trip. However, the platforms and the tools that exist today allow for us to market and communicate directly to people like never before in the digital age we live in. Being a good marketer and communicator in the church allows you and your team to be a resource to the other ministries in the church.

Yes, you may be promoting specific church events, but church marketing is not just about some product or service. This is something far greater. We have the opportunity to communicate the greatest exchange there ever was. That should not be taken lightly. As a church marketer and communicator, God has entrusted you to tell His story and the story of the church you serve. Do not neglect the magnitude of this. I understand that some of you are facing a conflicting situation where the pastor or other leadership may not see the importance of this, that maybe you have to even fight for a website or to start a Facebook page. I also understand that some of you are volunteers who are a one-man band doing this out of the goodness of your heart while you juggle a full-time job, a family, or both.

Marketing is messy. Ministry is messy. Combine the two together and it can get overwhelming. Your church, your ministry, and even how your marketing and communications plans are approached may not match what the mega churches are doing (we'll discuss this at greater length later on). Being a part, volunteering, and working with churches of all sizes has allowed me to see this. I thank God for allowing me to be a part of different church environments and situations just to be able to see church marketing in this perspective.

Now that we've discussed what this book is, let's talk about what it is not. This book isn't a step-by-step tutorial book. It will not be filled with the how-to's on how to get the most likes on your Facebook page, how to setup an Instagram page, how to upload a YouTube video, or how to design a sermon series graphic in Photoshop. Although, I would love to show you tutorials on how to accomplish your church projects well. This book is not a letter to your pastor or leader to tell them how to run your church. This book is not meant to shove ideas or a strategy plan that gives definitive quantifiable results for you and your church. This book is not meant to destroy everything your church has ever done and tell you that you are wrong. However, that does not mean you keep doing things the way you have always done them. Be willing to be stretched and try new things. This book is not a formula book. This book is not an if-then statement: If you do this at your church, then you will get this many people there on a Sunday morning or any other event.

There is no right way to do church. There is no right way to do marketing. Combine the two together and there is no right way to do church marketing. You have to determine what works for your church, for your ministry, for the people God has surrounded you with. That's why this book is open ended. This book summarizes what I have learned church marketing is and how to make it simple to keep your mind on track with each project. I want this book to lead you to ask more questions. I want this book to lead you to leap and try new things. To dig in more to what God has called you to. I believe that it is when we are unphased and ask the bigger questions that we are led to the discovery of greater answers.

Since bigger questions lead to great answers, that is why I have structured and broken down this book segmented by questions. These questions are simple but mighty. I began asking these questions when I started designing graphics projects. These are the questions I still ask because every client understands them, they give you the answers you need, and it is a fool-proof framework every time for every project. These questions are who, what, where, when, why, and how. These questions are the basic framework of writing that every elementary school student learns at some point early in their education. Who is in your story, what is taking place, where is it taking place, when is it taking place, why is it happening, and how is it happening. Loving to write since an early age, I took these questions to heart when I would write my class creative short stories in elementary school. When I faced my early design projects, I soon realized that clients, leaders, pastors, or whoever I was working with did not always give me all the details and information needed to complete a project. With still learning Photoshop, Illustrator, and trying to be creative enough to figure out how to create something that actually looked decent and pleased the client, I knew I did not have time to go back and forth with the client to drag the information. Now, side note, this isn't the fault of who you are working with. They often don't know the information you need and may not even have full clarity on what the details actually are; that's often why they are coming to you. This is the point of why it is vital to have a framework with simple questions to go back to and ask.

We are living in a time where we are in the biggest communication shift in history. Your church refusing to change its ways, methods, or strategies could be detrimental to the health of your church. It is not a matter of whether your church needs a website or not. It is not a matter of whether your church needs a social network account or not. It is a matter of how your church lives in the 21st Century. We live in a world where the resources are endless to where the smallest church can have a platform on the same level as a giant corporation. How will you use the resources that are being used by corporate marketers and communicators? How will the church adapt? How do you reach a dying and lost world? How do you fulfill the Great Commission in the 21st Century? What is the purpose and goals of a church marketer? How does marketing help the church? How does a church marketer serve the church?

In developing the right framework for what this book needs to be, I sat down and thought of the general information I typically needed for a project whether it was a logo, website, event promotion, etc. and I remember this simple writing framework that my teachers ingrained in me during elementary school. For example, if you have a student ministry event coming up that needs to be promoted at church, who's this event for, what is the event, when is the event, where is the event, how is the event happening, and why is the event happening? These questions give answers that explain the information that must be communicated directly to the audience and, indirectly, the promotional design/pieces. These questions became the framework for this book. When we, as marketers, can keep it this simple, it becomes simple for our ministry leaders, pastors, and volunteers to grasp and implement as well.

On the cover of this book, you'll notice the stained-glass window icon. Six sections on each side of the window. One section for each question of this book with the cross in the center. The church I was raised in was filled with stained-glass windows. When you looked in or out of those windows, there was an added dimension of beauty by seeing things in different colors. Different colors and imperfect sized pieces coming all together to create a beautiful piece of art while serving its purpose as a window. What a picture of what the Church is designed to be. A window is not meant to be dirty and fogged up. It is harder to see through it. A window is meant to be kept clean to see in and out of it clearly. Church marketing is as simple as a window. Church marketing is not meant to become fogged up but is meant to be kept simple and clear. With the cross in the center of it all, church marketing can be made simple. When it is made simple, it allows the lost world to see inside the window catching a glimpse of the beauty of the church and also allows the church to see the lost world outside the window that is waiting to hear the Gospel.

Thank you, church marketer and communicator, for what you do, your willingness, your commitment, your love, and your passion. I pray this book leads you to ask even bigger questions. I pray this book encourages you to follow this calling in ministry. I pray this book provides you with a framework you can apply in your own church and ministry to market with purpose. I pray this book helps you overcome this feeling of being overwhelmed and simplifies things for you. We do not have time to be caught up in feeling overwhelmed because we have the greatest story to tell—the story of redemption. Let's walk together in this ministry marketing journey.

CHAPTER 2
WHO?
WHO ARE YOU?

We are a culture obsessed with discovering ourselves. We feel like we must label everything. Personality tests, enneagram, strength tests, color tests, spirit animal tests, sibling birth order tests, the list goes on. There are tests everywhere that will give you a questionnaire and display results that help you better define and detail exactly who you are. I have nothing against these tests, as I have taken a good many over the years and have found that many of these tests further confirm what I already knew about myself.

However, if I gave your church a personality questionnaire, how would the results describe who you are as a church?

Exercise: Describe your church, as a collective body of believers, in one sentence.

Being able to definitively declare who you are as an organization, as a body of believers, as a church, announces to the world your establishment and who you are on track to be. Proclaiming this inside the church gives your people something tangible to adhere to. It provides a sense of direction for where your people should be going. Yes, the Church is the body and, yes, Jesus is the head of the Church, but that does not mean we sit idly by at the local churches with no type of leadership and no sense of direction of who we are and where we are headed.

Knowing who you are as a local church, your identity, is the foundation of knowing the rest of the who, what, when, where, why, and the how framework. Knowing who you are as a church establishes your purpose, your why. While it is important to know your purpose, your 'why', at the beginning when establishing who you are as a church, we will focus on the 'why' specifically in the final chapters of this book for the sake of bringing it all back around full circle to who you are and what your purpose is as a local church helping you bring greater clarity to your church marketing plan.

Living in a world where people are more confused than ever about their own identities requires the Church to be firm in their identity now more than ever. Before we get down to the nitty gritty of describing who you are as a local church, we first need to summarize who the Church is. Notice I said the Church, with a capital C. The big Church. The global Church.

At the heart of it, the Church is the global body of Christ followers. As Paul writes to the Ephesians, the Church is "built on the foundation of the apostles and prophets, with Christ Jesus Himself as the chief cornerstone" (Ephesians 2:20, NIV). The fact that Jesus is the head of the Church unites us. I believe that God is calling His Church to be more unified than ever in this divided world we live in.

In his letter to the local church in Corinth, Paul appeals to the Corinthians to "agree with one another in what you say and that there be no divisions among you, but that you be perfectly united in mind and thought" (1 Corinthians 1:10, NIV). If the Church cannot be unified and your local church specifically cannot be unified, then who can be in this world?

It's important to know who the Church is and who the Church belongs to because we've missed the point if we don't know. The mission and the vision of the Church is centered around Jesus Christ and His Kingdom. If it's not, then the Church has missed the point. If it's not, then the Church is failing and must get back under the head, who is Jesus.

While the Church is the global community of Christ followers, there are thousands upon thousands of local churches that gather together across the world. Every local church is given a unique purpose, which aligns to the overall mission and vision of the global Church.

There is a reason that God has established numerous local churches across our regions and our world. It's because it takes them all to reach the vast number of people God has created with a variety of similarities and differences. Not every local church can reach every person in the world or even every person in your community. We'll talk about this deeper in discussion in the next chapter and how your audience relates to your 'who.'

Who are you as a local church though? What's your brand? When I say that word 'brand', some of you may be turned off because you are not Apple or Disney or Nike or any other big brand that's easily recognizable by its logo. That's where I want to be very clear: your logo is not your brand. Your logo is not who you are. If we're talking about logos, then know that your logo is supposed to reflect who you are, not define who you are.

In early 2018, I received a call from a pastor from the church I interned at during high school and part of college. At the time of the call, almost one year had passed since I had stepped down as an intern from this church in an effort to focus more on my freelance business and college.

During this phone call, the pastor expressed how the church had really shifted its mission, vision, and purpose after undergoing leadership changes, including the calling of a new senior pastor just a few months prior. With this rebrand they wanted a new logo that reflected who they were and this mission and vision the leadership believed God had given them moving forward, and they wanted me to design it.

Side note: This turned into doing more than just the logo, but taking on the rest of the rebrand, and eventually being hired as the Director of Marketing and Communications.

When I design a new logo for an organization, I first consult with them to gain insight as to who they are as an organization. If they cannot answer their 'who', I send them back to the drawing board before I can get started on the logo. Why? When you look at the logos that have stood the test of time, it is because they reflect who their company is, even if it is a small piece of symbolism in the logo design.

Even though I was very familiar with this church, I still asked them the same initial questions (who, what, where, when, why, and how) to ensure they knew who they were in this rebrand and to gain more insight about what the logo needed to include. As a result, not only did the finished logo come out clean and good looking, but it resulted in a logo that tells a story. It reflects who the church is in their mission, vision, and purpose.

A logo is important for marketing because it attaches a visual aid that connects a message to an organization/person. Remember, an effective logo reflects who you are instead of defining who you are. In the strategy and marketing processes, the logo does not come first. Knowing who you are must come first, before any strategies are created and any logos are thought about.

Designing new logos and participating in rebrand projects for clients involves creating a set of brand guidelines. The brand guidelines are a file compiled by me that includes the fonts, colors, specific ways to use and not use the logo, and more. Before I include any of that though, the first page answers two questions: "What's a brand?" and "Why does it matter?"

Here are examples of what I write in response to those questions and deliver to a client:

What's a brand?

A brand is not a logo. A brand consists of atmospheres, experiences, cultures, images, and words. Ultimately, a brand consists of who you are and what you are about. When people hear the words of YOUR CHURCH, what do they think of? That is part of your brand. While we cannot change or control people's perceptions, what can we manage and control is in our presentation.

Why does it matter?
These brand guidelines are not just a list of rules. Rather, they are standards that will assist in communicating the mission, vision, and appearance of your organization clearly and consistently.

Your brand is more than your logo. Your brand is deeper than your appearance. It reflects who you are. What do people think about when they see your church's logo? What do people think about when they hear your church name? Your brand speaks to who you are.

When I ask, "who are you?" I want to know more than just your church's name. That's easy. Your church's 'who' involves digging deep into that name. What's the mission? What's the vision?

Think about it. If I asked you who you are, you would tell me your name. As the conversation progressed though, you would tell me your likes, dislikes, interests, goals, passions, your family, where you are from. Pretty soon I would have a well-rounded idea and knowledge of who you are. I would know the person behind your name.

Your name is simply your identifier, which only scratches the surface of who you are. Getting to know you is getting to discover all about you. The same goes for a church, or any organization for that matter. The church's name is just the identifier at the surface. It does not tell me who the church is. I have to get to know it. You have to get to know your church to be able to market and communicate who you are as a church.

Vision and mission statements define your church's 'who.' Putting a vision and mission in front of people motivates people. Just telling people your church's name does not motivate people. Putting vision and purpose (mission) in front of them motivates them because they can attach themselves to it. People desire to know how they can be a part. If the Church is the community of believers, then the believers must know how they can be a part and what their purpose is in that specific community of believers at your church.

At its core, a vision statement declares who you want to become. What are you working toward? What are your goals? Your vision statement influences everything you do as a church because this is what you are working toward. Do not make your vision statement easily attainable though. Let it be lofty.

The vision statement is what your church desires for the future state of your church to look like. The vision is something that the church is working toward. It is answering who you desire to be in the future as a church.

A mission statement simply describes your church's priorities and values. Your mission details your purpose. It details why you exist. We'll go into further detail into how your 'who' connects to your 'why' in chapter 9. A mission statement is meant not only to detail the future direction of your church in a broad sense, but it is also meant to be a reminder to your people why you exist.

Whether or not it has been stated verbally or written down, your church has a mission statement. Think about it. Why does your church exist? What is your purpose? What are your values? What are your priorities? Where are you headed? What is your church's business? Your mission statement is your statement of purpose. Your church's mission statement should reveal who you want to be and who you want to serve. It's defining your 'who'.

Exercise: Go online, search some of the largest corporations you can think of and look at their mission statements. It's not meant to be overcomplicated. It's meant to serve as a reminder to your people and to even those on the outside to see why you exist.

Even the Church has a mission statement: the Great Commission. "Therefore go and make disciples of all nations, baptizing them in the name of the Father and of the Son and of the Holy Spirit, and teaching them to obey everything I have commanded you." - Matthew 28:19-20 NIV

It communicates the broad sense of the future direction we are headed, going into all nations. It tells our values, our priorities, and our purpose of making disciples, baptizing them, and teaching them. Our mission is to go, make, baptize, and teach.

Let's be clear: as a local church, your vision and mission statements should not steer too far from this overall vision of what God designed the church to be and the global Church mission statement. If it does, then your church has missed it. Go back to the drawing board!

That may sound harsh, but we have to quit worrying about our individual church names and focus on the name of Jesus! When the mission and the vision of the Church, and that includes individual local churches, is anything other than Jesus Christ, then we have missed it as Christ followers.

That's even hard for me to say because in marketing we are strategizing how to promote the name above everything else. How do we lift up the name of an organization? How do we build the brand of an organization? How do we make an organization renown and recognizable by as many people as possible?

However, in church marketing, you are promoting a name that's greater than your local church's name. Your church is and should be lifting up the name of Jesus more than any other name. Jesus is who you are lifting up. If you are doing that, that becomes a part of your brand. That's what makes not only Jesus but your local church renown and recognizable.

As local churches, your church's 'who' must put Jesus above your church's own individual name. Your church's 'who' must proclaim Jesus louder than your church's name and location.

While you are defining your 'who,' you must ask yourself, "Are we trying to make a name only for ourselves or are we trying to name for our Savior?" When you focus on the name of Jesus before your church's own name, your church's 'who' cannot be any better.

When organizations begin, the first thing often done is establishing the 'who,' and that involves establishing the vision and mission of the organization. Defining the 'who' is often referred to as the first step of starting a successful organization because without it the organization can easily find itself in an identity crisis.

If an organization does not know who it is, then it cannot know what it is supposed to do, or where it is supposed to go, and who it is supposed to serve. Not knowing the 'who' makes you idle.

Knowing the 'who' is essential for marketing because in marketing planning everything needs to connect back to the 'who.' If you are sitting idle by not knowing your 'who,' then how can anything be marketed? If it does not fit in the vision statement or the mission statement, then it does not fit who you are and cannot be properly marketed.

In marketing, one of the essentials to know is a SWOT analysis. This analysis identifies the Strengths, Weaknesses, Opportunities, and Threats (SWOT) of an organization. Strengths and weaknesses are internal factors. This means that they are factors that can be controlled by the organization itself. Opportunities and threats, on the other hand, are external factors. These are out of the organization's control.

Why is it important to know this? It's important to know what you are good at and where you are lacking. While you cannot control the opportunities and threats, it is important to know what you are facing.

So, in your church's 'who', it is essential to know your strengths and weaknesses because these factors influence who you are and what you are about in your past, present, and future.

Have you ever known someone without ever actually being introduced to that person? Maybe someone else told you about this person and who they were. Now, sometimes this information you receive about who a person is may be true and sometimes, unfortunately, the information you receive is false.

The same goes for churches across the world. What the world portrays about the Church is typically false. So why do we allow the world too often dictate the narrative of the Church and tell people who we are?

If you want the people of the world or your community to know who the Church really is and who your local church really is, then you need to take over the narrative and tell the story.

If you don't tell your community and the world who you are as a church, then someone else will, and I cannot promise that it will be the truth and reveal who your church is.

Knowing your church's 'who' communicates that your church is secure in its identity. Remember that our identity is in Christ and without Him we are nothing. Jesus is the pulse of the Church. If Jesus is not the one breathing life into your church, then your church is either dead or in a dying state.

Jesus makes it clear why our identity must be rooted in Him. Jesus said, "I am the vine; you are the branches. If you remain in me and I in you, you will bear much fruit; apart from me you can do nothing" (John 15:5, NIV).

Our 'who' is rooted in Him. We are the branches that grow from the vine, Him. As the Church, we must remain in Him. If we do, we will bear fruit. If not, then we cannot do anything.

Growing up, a phrase I often heared from my family and family friends was, "Remember who you are and whose you are." As a church, you must remember who you are and whose you are. Without that, there is no way to move forward and do anything. Without knowing and remembering this, your church's marketing plan is flat and nonexistent. Your church cannot proclaim to a dying world it needs to belong to Jesus if your church does not know who they are.

CHAPTER 3
WHO?
WHO'S YOUR ONE?

Not too long ago, I designed a sermon series entitled, "Advocate". The premise of this series was challenging people to discover who their one person was and to pray for them. Who was the one person who they knew that needed Jesus and needed to be saved? To make this series interactive and to get the congregation on board and participating with this challenge, the pastor asked me to make cards to be placed in the seatbacks of the chairs for the congregation. The card had the series artwork on it and the word 'advocate'. Underneath the word advocate was the question, "Who's your one?" and a blank line under it for a person's name to be written.

Exercise: Think deeper about this. Let the magnitude of this sermon hit you when you think about what our world would be like if all Christians prayed for salvation each day for at least one person. You alone might not be able to change the whole world by yourself, but you could help change one person's world.

As I prepared for the Sunday service when the challenge would be given, I moved down each aisle and each row of seats placing each card with care. In that worship center in the church, silence filled the room with only the sound of me sorting the cards and the cards rubbing against the fabric of the seat pocket. It was in those silent moments and handling the hundreds of cards that it hit me that there would be names, real names, written on each of these blanks. When I drew the line on the card in Adobe Illustrator, it was just a straight line being drawn. However, in this moment, the line on each card was not on the computer screen but in my hands. In a matter of days, that line would have handwritten letters resting on that line, which formed a name of a person that needed to be saved. It was in that moment that God reminded me those were not nearly seven hundred cards but that they were nearly seven hundred names of people that needed to step from death to life. There were nearly seven hundred people in desperate need of a Savior who needed people praying for them. I may not have known those names specifically, not even the pastor would know them all individually. However, God knew each name and He knew what they needed.

I kept an extra card in my Bible and left the line blank to remember that a name went there. A name I may not know specifically, but a name that needs Jesus and that He already calls by name.

Exercise: So, before we go any further, I want you to think of someone. A familiar face. Family. Friend. Whoever it may be. Now, I want you to really picture that person in your mind. Think of every detail you know about that person. What they like or don't like. What their story is. What their relationship is to you. What made you think of this person first. Now, call them by name. You likely know a great amount about this person that you are picturing. By knowing them, you know how to reach them. You know how to communicate with them. Why? Because that relationship has been built. The only way to keep reaching them is to keep getting to know them. To stay in touch. To be with them. To let them know you are there. It is not a hard concept. It is something we do every day with the people we know and love. The people we intentionally build relationships with.

If it is this simple though, why do we make things complicated when we think about the word audience? When we think of the audience, we think of standing on a stage and looking out in the masses of the crowd that stares back at us. Faces may me blurred. Faces may be dimmed. Those people may not be known. However, when the spotlight focuses down on one face, on one person, then a name can be known. A relationship can be built. Likes, dislikes, interests, disinterests, stories can become unearthed and discovered.

It's easy to say people need Jesus. It's easy to say people need to read their Bible more. It's easy to say this group of people needs to be in church. It's easy to say we need "this many" people to fill the seats and pew of our churches. In these broad statements, the 'people' are still blurred out faces. These people are still just a broad statement.

One of my greatest joys is to meet new guests at my church at our Guest Services desk. Every person that comes to that desk has a different background, a different story, a different path of how they came to church for the first time. In those moments of new guests filling out connection cards, I can learn their name, what brought them to our church campus, and what they are looking for. Attaching that name turns that guest from a number into a name making them known. When I am sitting at my desk planning out social media posts, or event promotion, or email campaigns, I think of those names— guests and members alike—and see their faces. When you can picture your audience clearly, you can clarify who your church needs to reach.

Once you have figured out who you are, you have to figure out who your audience is. Who you are means nothing if you do not know who you are trying to reach. The two go hand in hand. Why? When we go back to the mission, the vision, and the purpose of your church, there are people tied to that.

My church's mission statement is to "saturate the world with the

Good News." Now, let's illustrate this mission statement. This church has a big glass of water. This water is unlike any normal water because it is living water. It makes everything it touches grow. If it touches dry ground, it restores the cracks in the cracked dirt and nourishes the soil. If it touches a withering flowering, the flower is restored to its beautiful form. If it touches fading grass, it renews its greenness. This water gives life. Newness. Refreshment. However, it cannot be what it needs to be to restore the soil, the withering flower, or the fading grass if the water is not poured out of the glass. We know what the water is and what the water has the ability, strength, and power to do, yet we keep it inside the glass. Keeping it inside the glass keeps from the multiplication of growth that could be seen in the fields that lay before us.

Jesus is the Living Water. The Living Water is to be poured on out onto this Earth. There are people with cracks in their foundations who need to be healed and nourished. There are people withering away. There are people fading. What if they knew there was a water source that could restore them? This is your audience. For His Church, She has the most beautiful audience. An audience comprised of people that need Jesus. That need their soil, flowers, and grass watered. You see, the purpose must be foundationally tied to who you are to reach who you need to reach. It all goes back to answering the who. Who's your audience?

According to the American Marketing Association, marketing is defined as, "the activity, set of institutions, and processes for creating, communicating, delivering, and exchanging offerings that have value for customers, clients, partners, and society at large." Attached to the last part of that phrase are the words "for customers, clients, partners, and society at large." Marketing is for a certain group of people. It's an exchange of value for people, from people. Who are your people? Who is your church for? From a biblical perspective, this marketing definition could be written as "the activity and processes for creating, communicating, delivering, and exchanging offerings that have eternal value for both believers and non-believers."

What value is your church offering? How are you creating, communicating, delivering, and exchanging this value? Does your audience know why they should join you? When big corporations sit down to answer these same questions about their audience, many enlist the assistance of the industry's best market researchers to discover everything they can about the intended audience and further segment them.

Audience segmentation divides your audience using certain metrics. Audience segmentation has been used in the marketing industry for decades as target audience identification has the potential to either make or break an entire marketing strategy. Successfully identifying a target audience through segmentation guides marketers how to best reach their intended audience in the most efficient and effective way possible. You may have heard of demographics, geographics, psychographics--enter audience segmentation. These audience segmentations help build an audience profile that details who the majority of the people you are attempting to reach. While you probably do not have the bountiful budget to hire the industry's best market researchers to help you identify and segment your church's target audience, you can still successfully segment who makes up your church's congregation and surrounding community. To better understand these metrics, let's break them down.

Demographics
What are the general characteristics of your targeted audience? What is their average age, gender, marital status?

This does not mean you should pass out a questionnaire in

your church one Sunday and require everyone to answer like they are sitting in the DMV. This is basic information that can be collected along the way. These are the more tangible characteristics. For example, have your guests fill out a connection card that details this basic information. If you do not want to sort through spreadsheets and databases of all your church guests' and members' information, then do not neglect the power of observation. Walk around your church one Sunday. Look at the people that surround you and walk by you. Is your church primarily made of older people? Younger people? Married families? Observe and identify the demographics of the people you encounter.

Geographics
Where does your targeted audience live?

I was born, raised, and still live in the Bible Belt in Georgia. The church I was raised in is less than five minutes from my home. You have to make only one turn onto a different road to get to this church. I love the story of how my family came to be a part of this church. When my grandmother (my Ma) was five years old, she, her parents, and sister were forced to change churches due to road access being cut off to reach their current church. The solution was to attend the church that just was down the street and in their actual community that had been planted and continued to be filled with family members and family friends. Now this could be a longer story, but the point of sharing this story is that my family's place of worship was affected by geographic location.

Today on my street, I could access at least three, if not five, churches in less than five minutes. I lose count of how many churches I pass on my way to my church. We do not have a shortage of churches in northeast Georgia. First and foremost, I am grateful for this because it is not the case in other parts of the country and the world. It is important to know where people in your church live. How far are they commuting to attend? For many churches, understanding the geographic segmentation can determine where satellite campuses should be placed to better reach their audience. For your church, maybe you want to launch small, off-campus groups. Where are the best places in your area to launch those? Geographic segmentation can help with that.

Psychographics

What are the attitudes, interests, hobbies, and preferences of your target audience?

Different from the tangible characteristics discovered with demographics, psychographics deal more with the intangible characteristics of your intended audience. What are the people you are trying to reach doing outside of church? What is their lifestyle like? I once sat in a small group where we were discussing the importance of sharing your faith and inviting people to church. During the conversation, one lady spoke out and said, "I had to realize that my lifestyle will not reach everybody and allow me to share my faith with everyone that I come in contact with." She described someone she knew with a body full of tattoos who was part of a motorcycle group. This completely contrasted with who she was. Her attempt to share Jesus with this person did not go quite as planned because it was difficult for her to relate with this person, to find common ground, to find the open door of opportunity to insert Jesus. She shared that this person did eventually meet Jesus and is now part of a church that is dedicated to motorcycle groups. It was not until this person met people with similar interests and lifestyles that they were able to be receptive to hearing the Gospel message and eventually attend church. Psychographic segmentation allows you to know your population on an individual level.

Psychographics can help plan out certain ministry events because it helps you know better what to provide at the event. For example, if your men's ministry is full of men that are avid hunters, then a golf outing will not appeal to many men in your church. Yes, you are trying to share the Gospel with people, but the church is involved in discipleship making. Discipleship is relational. Relationships are built in finding common ground. Common ground is only found when you are willing to get to know the actual person and what interests them.

Audience segmentation need not be confused with being discriminatory in any way shape or form based on gender, age, race, location, or even interests. In fact, it can become dangerous for a church when part of your audience is forgotten and only one part of your audience is reached. God has placed your church in a specific location close to specific people with specific lifestyles for a specific reason. Unless your church is a church plant, rarely are you going to get to handpick your audience from an assembly line to create the ideal audience that is the easiest to market to.

For example, with an established product like the iPhone, Apple understands that they will never win over every Android user and vice versa. Churches and church marketers, you must be okay with the fact that your church will not win everyone over. Not everyone will attend your church. Not everyone will like your church better than their own. That's okay. This is why there are so many local churches established in our nation and our world. The Church is better when we can divide and conquer.

Even if your church audience is not the ideal model that the blogs, books, and videos portray, that does not give you permission to neglect them and set out on your own trail to reach the audience you want. In my experience, the area where I have sadly seen this the most is neglecting age in the church. Let's call it the age divide. I have had the privilege to be a part of churches during my lifetime that have had great age variance, meaning the church population was well distributed across multiple generations. In marketing, the more age groups you start adding into an audience the broader the marketing must get. In the church, I understand and have witnessed congregations growing older and having to grasp to reach the younger generations to keep their church alive. I understand the circle of life aspect. You have to have young people and young families in your church to keep your church growing. Unfortunately, I have witnessed churches though that have cast the older generation off, pulling the rug out from underneath them all in an effort to 'reach' the young people.

I read an article recently about a church asking their members of a certain age to leave in an attempt to reorganize and reach only young people. These older church members were distraught because they felt as if they had lost their homes. If an older generation still exists in your church, then they are still a part of your audience. Will they require you to change your methods a bit in how you market to them? Yes, but marketing is not about your personal preference. Marketing is about satisfying the needs and wants of your audience.

I guarantee that there are people sitting in your pews and seats right now in your church campus that feel like they are not connected. They feel like they do not belong. They feel like they do not matter. Make your audience feel like they matter to your church. Let the audience know that you know who they are.

No matter what you do, certain aspects of your audience cannot be ignored. In the book of James, James writes about the dangers of partiality.

> My brothers, show no partiality as you hold the faith in our Lord Jesus Christ, the Lord of glory. [2] For if a man wearing a gold ring and fine clothing comes into your assembly, and a poor man in shabby clothing also comes in, [3] and if you pay attention to the one who wears the fine clothing and say, "You sit here in a good place," while you say to the poor man, "You stand over there," or, "Sit down at my feet," [4] have you not then made distinctions among yourselves and become judges with evil thoughts? [5] Listen, my beloved brothers, has not God chosen those who are poor in the world to be rich in faith and heirs of the kingdom, which he has promised to those who love him? [6] But you have dishonored the poor man. Are not the rich the ones who oppress you, and the ones who drag you into court? [7] Are they not the ones who blaspheme the honorable name by which you were called? [8] If you fulfill the royal law according to the Scripture, "You shall love your neighbor as yourself," you are doing well. [9] But if you show partiality, you are committing sin and are convicted by the law as transgressors.
>
> - James 2:1-9 (ESV)

Initially, I asked you to think about "who's your one?" Even the one matters in your church because the one matters to God. In Matthew, Jesus Himself even said, "What do you think? If a man owns a hundred sheep, and one of them wanders away, will he not leave the ninety-nine on the hills and go to look for the one that wandered off?" (Matthew 18:12, NIV). Knowing the one allows for you to get to know your audience as a whole. It allows you to shut the back door of your church and to get to know your church family as actual people not numbers.

It's important to let your audience know that they matter in order to help cultivate a non-consumerist culture. In being true to marketing, it could be easy to create a cookie-cutter church for people that satisfies that every need and want. Companies try to do it all the time with the products and services they offer. However, church is different in that church is not a product or service; church is a group of people. At my parents' and brother's church, as a church congregation they recite a worship manifesto. My favorite line in this recitation is, "we are here to be worshipers, not consumers." As a church marketer, remind yourself of this. Yes, you are trying to identify and reach a certain audience. However, remember that you are not selling a product or service. You are inviting them to be a living body part of a living body. In his letter to the Church of Corinth, Paul reminds the Corinthians that "now you are the body of Christ, and each of you is a part of it" (1 Corinthians 12:27, NIV). Does your entire audience know that they are a part of your church? Do the individual people know that they matter? It's important to know who your one is because the body does not function correctly when missing even the smallest piece.

Identifying your church target audience does not give you the license to neglect certain people. It does not give you the authority to lift certain people up on a pedestal either. Considering your 'who' allows you to better reach John that sits on the third row from the back in the far, left corner. Knowing who's your one allows you to better get to know who Susan that serves in children's ministry is. Considering your 'who' allows you to turn your numbers into names and to think of your congregation as not a number of people but as a family of names. Considering your 'who' allows you to remind and invite people to be a part of the mission that God has called you as a collective body of believers to.

CHAPTER 4
WHAT?
WHAT PLATFORMS?

Instead of us exclaiming 'lions, and tigers, and bears, oh my!', marketers and communicators exclaim 'social media, and websites, and podcasts, and videos, and apps', and the list goes on. All of these platforms are creating a space to share your message, your 'what.' Churches have the greatest 'what', the greatest message, to share so we need to be intentional of what platforms to share on. Everywhere we turn a new platform is taking the world by storm, beckoning us to learn it, love it, and live it immediately at the risk of losing our audience.

Picture an ocean and picture yourself in the ocean bobbing up and down being carried by the waves. Eventually you can get ready for the waves, allowing them to carry you a certain distance. However, it seems like there is always that one wave, or at least in my experience, that comes out of nowhere and knocks you down when you least expect it.

I imagine platforms a lot like this with platforms being like the waves. Eventually you can learn about certain platforms and be prepared for the way they exist and function. However, just when you think you have a platform nailed down, it seems like there is an algorithm change, or that platform is no longer relevant, leaving you knocked down and drenched by the water.

The vast number of platforms can be overwhelming because it will seem like you have to sort everything out with a specific plan of action, leaving no room for failure. The greater the platform presence, the more managing on your part is required. Let's be honest, if you fail on a platform, people will see it no matter what platform you are using. You're always susceptible to being knocked down by the wave. At the end of the day, you are more than likely a one-man band at your church doing this all alone, without an extensive team, that can be dedicated to only certain platforms. There is no separate web manager, social media manager, or email marketing specialist. There's you and only you. Because there's only you, it may feel easier not to learn any new platforms and just stick with the ones you know. However, are you willing to risk losing your audience and relevance over this?

Before we can even think about where to share, we must learn what a platform is and what platforms even exist. At the foundational level, what is a platform? A platform is something a message/person is positioned on allowing the message/person to be better heard and better seen. A platform amplifies communication. It is important to not confuse a platform with your message. A platform is not the end goal, but it gives an elevated position to your message. While a multitude of platforms exist, it is important to remember to keep your message consistent across each one you use. The platforms may change and evolve in the years to come, but the message never will.

Because your message is never changing as a church marketer, do not let your platforms command your message. Your message dictates the platforms, not the other way around. At its core, the Church is a living platform for the Gospel. The Church amplifies the Gospel. Each person in your church is a walking platform not only for your local church, but also for the Gospel.

Understanding what a platform is at a basic level allows you to better analyze specific platforms and determine what they are and how they can help amplify your church's message. Don't feel like you have to become a viral Internet sensation overnight across ten digital platforms. In platform building and sharing, take it one step at a time. There are two sides to every platform: production and consumption. On every platform, there is a production side that allows you to produce the content being shared on the specific platform and then there's the function of consumption that is literally allowing for the consumer to consume the content you have produced on the platform. Take the time to learn about the platform production and the platform consumption, one step at a time.

While we're learning about platforms, we must also consider the distinction between traditional and digital platforms. It's a well-known fact that we live in a digital world and that some digital marketing tactics have overtaken traditional marketing tactics. However, traditional platforms cannot be thrown to the wind just because we live in a digital world. Why? Because churches use the most basic traditional platform every week: a person on a stage, speaking to an audience (aka the pastor and the sermon). While you as the church marketer may not be the pastor sharing on this traditional platform (or maybe you are the pastor and all things marketing), this traditional platform must be considered in how this is sharing the Gospel message and your individual church's message.

At the church where I work as Director of Marketing and Communications, one of my favorite aspects of my job is being part of our Membership Class. There are many reasons why I loved being a part of this class to connect with new members, but for the purpose of this chapter, there was one specific part of the Membership Class that I love. In the beginning of the class, we review the "Ways We Can Communicate" (as I call it). In this section of the Membership Class, I reviewed which digital platforms our church was present on and how they could connect with us via these platforms. People cannot connect on a platform if they don't know you are present on the platform. One short page in the Membership Class booklet overviews each platform category we use and what we do on them. I found the benefits two-fold for this: (1) it allows all new members to see what platforms we used consistently and how to connect with us on them, and (2) it allows me to remember all the platforms we use and what they were to be used for.

So for the sake of this book, I translated this "Ways We Can Communicate" from the Membership Booklet, plus a few more additions, to make an overview of platforms for this book to help you categorize platforms and discover what they are to be used for. Reading this overview allows you to see, at a glance, what platforms are out there for you to learn about one step at a time and choosing what's best for your church.

What platforms? The Overview

Mobile Apps

Over the years mobile apps for churches have either been a hit or miss. In fact, I have discouraged churches from using them for years until recently. Before I tell what changed my mind, I must tell you why I discouraged churches from using them because maybe a mobile app is not for you and your church at the moment. And please know, that's okay!

(2) The upkeep. An app is like a home, it takes a lot of

maintenance to keep it looking nice. It always needs a fresh coat of paint, updated furnishings, pictures, etc. That takes time, so if you cannot dedicate the time to the upkeep, don't use this type of platform.

Now, what turned me on to mobile apps for churches, you might ask? A pandemic! You may have heard of it: COVID-19! In fact, I'm writing this while under a shelter-in-place order by my governor. You'll see more references to COVID-19's impact on this church marketing framework later on. But for now, back to church mobile apps!

Due to the coronavirus my church, like practically all other churches, had to move online. As we made the switch to an online presence, I had to redo most of our church website, which was aimed at reaching the church guest instead of at reaching the church member. For every ministry and their online resources, there was another website link. I felt like we were spouting off twenty different links to church members. It felt like, "For this, go to mychurch.org/this and for this, go to mychurch.org/this and for that, go to mychurch.org/that." It felt like an endless supply of links. If it seemed hard for me to keep up with, I knew it must be difficult for the church guest and church member. We had to have one platform to send our people to, where it would all be in one location as a hub.

Enter the mobile app. If we were at a place of taking church and worship directly to the people, then why not bring everything else directly to them all in one central location at their fingertips. A mobile app puts everything in one location and eases communication by now saying, "Go to our app to learn more or do this or watch this." From there, the app can redirect them to other platforms as needed.

Mobile app usage is on the rise as mobile device usage continues to increase in our society. People are using mobile apps every single day, so it should be a platform to consider and not be ignorant about. Even though I'm for the church mobile app now, it doesn't take away the cost and upkeep reservations. A mobile app may not be feasible right now, it may have to be something you work toward. If it's not for your church right now, that's okay. Do what works best for your people. But, if a mobile app is feasible for your church right now, really consider this platform as an option. Begin to think how this could benefit your church, your ministries, your connection.

Email

Email may be one of the oldest digital platforms on this list, but that doesn't negate its value to marketing and communications. Why? Well, email reaches a large group of people at once. It allows personalization while also reaching the masses. It also has few limits. No length limit for text and as for images/videos, just make sure they are under 20 MB (unless you use a link to your media in the email). Email is a platform that you own and can fully control. You are not bothered with algorithms or platform function changes/updates. Email is easy to use. Most people know how to use email and have an email address. It's yours to edit. You own it. In the church world, I use email for two purposes: for church wide communication and for targeted messaging.

For church wide communication, I'll use it for very specific events, reminders, or follow-ups. Church wide emails are how I also will send a church weekly newsletter, call it the digital church bulletin. For targeted messaging, you can use email to contact only specific groups and a list of people for certain events and ministries.

Starting an email distribution list is easy. Just ask people for their email address and their permission for you to send them emails and you're set. It does not take fancy software. It doesn't take a lot of prior knowledge to get started. It's just waiting for you to get started. Email may be one of the oldest digital platforms but it's still effective and any church can and should use it in their marketing and communications.

Text Messaging

Texting is like email. Everyone, for the most part, has it. Everyone, for the most part, knows how to use it. Texting is part of everyone's, for the most part, daily routine. Text messaging is now preferred over the phone call for many. Text messaging is quick and simple. Like email, it can reach the masses, or it can reach specific targeted groups. Its only limit is the number of characters. Make sure your message is short and sweet.

Starting a texting distribution list is easy like email. Ask people for their cell phone numbers and their permission for you to send them texts and you're set. A bit of quick advice though: If you're using this for church-wide communication, invest in a mass texting service that allows to you send out mass texts easily through a special code and not your personal phone number or any personal phone number. Leave the personal text messages to pastors, ministry leaders, and small group leaders.

Social Networks

Shoutout to the Facebookers, Tweeters, Instagrammers, YouTubers, TikTokers, and more! At this point, the question is probably not are you present on a social network, but which social network(s) are you present on. Like a mobile app, social networks take upkeep and time. It takes constant refreshers in content and interaction. Algorithms are constantly changing. Functions are constantly changing. Social networks are where the people are though, so it's well worth the effort. Your focus is to pick which one(s) best fit your audience. We'll talk more about this in our when/where chapter.

Whenever you do pick your social platform for your church, I suggest committing to one big one first, more than likely Facebook, unless your church is only teenagers. Like I said, social networks require upkeep. Your social network platforms thrive on quality and refreshed content and die on neglected and aged content.

Social platforms are like children. Rarely do they like all the same food (content), interact in the same way, like the same clothes (design), etc. Each social network has a different name and a different interface for a reason, because they are all different. Facebook owns Instagram, yet they behave different, look different, and interact with followers differently.

Keeping up with one platform and raising it well takes a great amount of time and effort. Keeping up with more than one platform takes even more time and effort. Again, it's up to you. How many can you commit to and which platform reaches the greatest portion of your church's audience?

Website

Your church needs a website. I repeat: your church needs a website. This is not a question anymore. This isn't the 1990s. A website is your church's digital front door. Most people will visit your church website before they even step foot in your church. You have one chance to make a first impression and, in today's world, that first impression will more than likely be made on your church's website. Your website should point people to your church, who you are, what you're about, and, most importantly, point people to Jesus.

Don't make people have to search far and wide for Jesus on your website.

I've designed websites for church, small businesses, and nonprofits. I've even given advice to churches, small businesses, and nonprofits about websites that I haven't designed. Yes, web designers are nice to have (I have to say that because I am a web designer), however, because of advancing technology websites are now more affordable and even easier to create. You don't have to break the bank to create a functional website that creates an influential digital front door to your church anymore.

Live Streaming

This was a last-minute addition. Why? Coronavirus. Live streaming is now easier than ever, thanks to advancing equipment and platforms. Yes, the more expensive equipment is nice and necessary in some cases. Yes, that equipment takes more money and people to implement and manage. However, we live in the world of powerful smartphones and streaming platforms like Facebook Live, YouTube, and our websites.

On these platforms, your smartphone could stand to reach as many people as the most expensive equipment can. Don't overlook live streaming as a platform just because you don't currently use it. Your church may not be at a point to use this platform every Sunday, but it's something to be prepared for because you never know when the opportunity for your church to meet in person may be stripped away and the church must go completely online.

Word of Mouth

One of the oldest and most effective marketing tactics has always been, probably always will be, word of mouth. Whether it's from the pulpit, the stage, video announcement, or person to person conversation, there is nothing like employing the word of mouth marketing tactic. Why?

Trust is a major factor in the success of word of mouth marketing. As a marketer, I could post Facebook ads all day long about why a guest should try Church A. While that will catch a several new faces, Bob and Jane don't trust a Facebook ad telling them why they should join Church A. Church A isn't going to publicize all of its problems, it's going to focus on the highlights. That's marketing 101 for you. However, John goes to Church A and is best friends with Bob and Jane. When he invites them to try Church A, they decide to come. Why? Because they trust John and his opinion. They know John.

The art of the invitation is not dead. In fact, I believe it's more alive than ever because people crave trusted sources of information today. The art of the invitation lives its best life through word of mouth because at the end of the day, people trust people.

Word of mouth may be overlooked as just common sense, but never overlook its power and influence in the marketing world. I have read countless textbooks and written numerous papers that attempt to explain why the power of word of mouth continues to maintain its strength over the years. In one sentence: Word of mouth marketing maintains its strong influence and power in the marketing world because it is a marketing tactic that connects itself to human nature. It connects itself to one of mankind's strongest tools, the mouth.

Once you familiarize yourself with what platforms are available and what platforms are best for your church to be present on, it's dangerous to then jump too far ahead. Don't forget to take this one step at a time. When I first started out in the church marketing world, being young and naive, I had this goal to be present on so many digital platforms including the top social networks at the time, by the end of my second week on the job. Remember how I said not to expect or feel like you have to become an overnight viral Internet sensation? Being present on a platform does not equate to succeeding on a platform. Being effective on a platform is what yields platform success.

If you don't want to feel overwhelmed by the number of platforms, take it one platform at a time. Taking the time to focus on one platform at a time allows you to get to know that platform like the back of your hand. It allows you to know the full functionality of the platform both on the production and consumption sides of things. By knowing the platform forward and backward, when the algorithm change or the platform-update wave crashes into you out of nowhere, you'll be able to know what hit you and recover faster. For example, if Facebook is a platform that your church needs to be using, then do not overwhelm yourself with any other platforms. Learn Facebook in and out. Learn how to produce engaging content on Facebook. Learn about your Facebook audience. Learn Facebook, Love Facebook, and Live Facebook. Once you feel comfortable letting the waves of Facebook carry you, another platform can be added.

While I give this advice to you, be aware that I know the platform situation will not always be cookie-cutter like this where you can get your Facebook page perfect before setting up an Instagram account that is verification-check-mark worthy. If you are like me, then you have probably inherited church platforms or church social accounts that require you to dive in headfirst and get involved in already established platforms. When I take over churches' social network accounts or help them establish social strategy plans, many already have created social network accounts on multiple social platforms. So how do you take it one step at time when you potentially must take the single steps on multiple platforms at a time? You must prioritize, find balance, and create consistency.

What platforms converge at the intersection of who your audience is and who you are as a church? The platforms that make the cut are the ones you confidently choose and push forward with in establishing a reputable presence. Whatever these platforms may be, you are committing to taking an active role and active voice. Don't choose a platform for the sake of showing the icon on your website. Choose the platforms that will connect your church.

In taking it one step at a time and learning a platform well, prioritize. In the world of social networks, you may not be able to create meaningful content consistently across all platforms. When choosing what platforms to share on, you have to be willing to prioritize what platforms hold the most value and will deliver the most value for the production and consumption of the platform.

Exercise: Similar to the list of categories and platforms I provided above, start your own list of platforms your church is present on. Now, in a separate column, write down the platforms you feel your church should be present on based on your audience, who you are as a church, and also what methods are popular right now. Looking at these two columns, are there any matches from the two platforms? On a separate piece of paper, write down the top three platforms you can commit to learn well and take an active role on these platforms. What is important about these platforms? How will these platforms further connect your church?

Now that you have prioritized your platforms, find balance. Finding balance is important because it helps with the sense of being overwhelmed. Are the platform's production and consumption being balanced? Not every ministry event, message, and promotion will be communicated through each platform you have a presence on. Choosing up front to find balance leads you to create consistency on each platform and to not spread yourself too thin.

The greatest danger in choosing what platforms to be present on is spreading yourself too thin because spreading yourself too thin builds to mediocrity. Spreading yourself too thin is a danger in the overall church marketing world, and even life itself. If you are overwhelmed as a church marketer, it's likely because you have spread yourself too thin. The greatest story I have ever heard about spreading yourself too thin came from a student conference breakout session. This lesson goes far beyond just choosing platforms in church marketing, this lesson is for you as an individual. A youth pastor was the leader of this breakout class for the entire week, and while I still have his notes on what he talked about, it was what he brought his wife in to say during the last session that still sticks with me. She talked about spreading yourself too thin in ministry and to illustrate she held two cups up. One cup full of water and one cup empty. She said in ministry we are constantly pouring out into empty cups. However, if we are never refilling our cups, we soon pour all of our water out in the empty cups leaving us to eventually empty ourselves. You cannot pour from an empty cup.

This is so true for the church marketing world and also ministry as a whole. Specifically speaking for platforms though, this is crucial to note. Being on more platforms does not make you successful if you cannot produce valuable content for consumption. When it comes to platforms and to answer the 'what' of church marketing, look for the platforms that will provide the most production and consumption value for the relationship between you, as the local church, and your members/community. More specifics on this to help you further narrow this answer down will come later on in answering the when, where, and the how. For now though, remember to take it one step at a time and do fewer platforms well to maintain a valuable presence instead of spreading yourself and your church too thin. Focus on what platforms effectively broadcast what message you are carrying and aiming to share.

CHAPTER 5
WHAT?
WHAT EQUIPMENT?

If you have been in ministry any amount of time, you know that the biggest hindrance in us moving forward in many areas is the budget, or the lack thereof. In the church world, the opportunity for frivolous spending is nonexistent. Many of you reading this book have likely taken on your church's marketing and communications department and formed it from the ground up as a volunteer. If salary is not in the question, a formal church marketing and communications line item in the budget is definitely not on the top five of the biggest ministry expenses in your church's budget. Trust me I understand church budgets. I understand budget requests and I understand hearing, "This money needs to be used here instead." And to a certain extent, be okay with that.

Every church will start somewhere. Not every church will have the multi-person team or the big salaries or the big budgets they can solely dedicate to marketing. That's where I have been able to step in with many churches and have found a great passion for helping churches because I have been there. I have worked with absolutely no budget to a decent budget that still has to be watched and carefully considered before any astronomical expenses are made.

However, I am here to tell you that your lack of budget should not, I repeat should not, stop you. Why? Because effective marketing and communications need not break the bank in the world that we live in today. It's not about having the best of the best or the most expensive, top of the line equipment. Having the best and the most expensive does not equal success. Having the greatest camera set up for your church's live stream does not guarantee you to have 1,000 or even 10,000 viewers on Facebook Live every Sunday. It's all about choosing what equipment is right for you: small prices, mighty power.

Because of the fast-paced technological advances we have seen in the last twenty years alone, it is safe to say that the playing field has been leveled in the marketing world. What do I mean by that? In decades prior, the huge corporations dominated the advertising and marketing world because they were the only ones that could afford the resources to do it effectively. Fast forward to 2020, it is not the lofty budgets or the luxurious equipment that make a video on YouTube go viral or gives a picture the most likes on Instagram.

The equipment you use need not break the bank because of the availability of consumer-friendly products that produce high quality results. We live in a user-generated content world now. In fact, the greatest piece of equipment you can ever have is sitting in your pocket: your smartphone. Some of the greatest gifts come in the smallest packages. From capturing, to editing, to publishing, your smartphone can do it all. With a piece of equipment like a smartphone, content can be shared in real time before it fades into irrelevant, old news. If you had to choose one piece of equipment to complete church marketing projects while on a deserted island, it would need to be your smartphone. It takes care of both the production and consumption sides of things, all at fingertips.

Quality does not just matter in digital equipment though, it is also something to consider in traditional marketing materials. Traditional signage still has its purpose in the world, including churches. If you have priced signage recently, you know that it can add up quickly. For an event I was working on, the church needed additional signage. In my initial signage scouting around the campus, it was easy to say a sign was needed here, a feather flag was needed there, and so on. However, things added up quickly and soon blew up the miniscule signage budget we had to work with. Going back to the drawing board to get signage under budget, I had to be strategic in the signage ordered because quality would definitely have to be chosen over signage quantity. It's the medium that is sharing your message, it has to be quality. Often your budget will halt a great deal of what you wish you could do, but it does force you to be creative and strategic about what equipment and platforms you use to gain the greatest reach in and around your church and community.

In the previous chapter about what platforms to choose and use, I said that there are two sides to platforms: production and consumption. What equipment you choose and use will impact your platform, your production, and what you produce will affect the consumption. What equipment should you choose? Equipment that supports the platforms you choose. A church was wanting to create a Venmo account to use as a payment method for an upcoming student event. Venmo was the perfect platform for this event: (1) it was a popular/ safe payment method, (2) it was a popular platform among students, (3) it was easy and mobile to use. The platform was set up. To track Venmo transactions made during the event, the plan was to have the app downloaded and monitored on an iPad to assure that proper transactions were being made and received on the platform. However, the issue hit when the Venmo app was tried to be downloaded on an older iPad that belonged to the church. The most-up to date Venmo app was incompatible with the iPad model. The solution for this was simple, by switching to another mobile device that was newer, thus making it compatible with the platform, the mobile payment platform was a huge success. While the problem was quick and easy to resolve, I share this uncomplicated example to show the bridge between what equipment you choose and what platforms you choose. If your equipment is incompatible with your platform, then neither production nor consumption can happen on your intended platforms.

In terms of choosing the right equipment, you don't have to have the best of the best, but you must measure quality versus quantity. While both quality and quantity have value, in my opinion, quality will almost always win over quantity. People (your audience) desire quality because of the vast quantity of content they are being thrown at in every direction. For example, in an endless scroll of hundreds of emails, most to be moved to trash without even being opened, what will make a person want to open your church's email instead of casting it off to the trash can like the others? Again, it is not about choosing the best, most expensive equipment. It is about choosing what will help you deliver the best quality content and your message (your what) on the platforms you have chosen. Quality over quantity.

Another crucial rule of thumb to remember when selecting equipment is to choose equipment you either already know how to use well or are committed to learning how to use well. I saw this lesson in action thanks to high school interns. In working as the Director of Marketing and Communications at a local church, I was gifted several high school interns from within the church's student ministry. This was a full circle moment for me as I was in that intern position just less than five years prior at that point and now, I was the mentor/supervisor. Our church needed content captured, both videos and pictures, of events for social media purposes and to overall build a photo library to have shareable content for our platforms. Two of the interns showed interest in photography and videography and, because I could not be at multiple places at once while also holding multiple cameras, showing interest in capturing was enough for me at that point (I told you, I understand the one-man band mentality). The first church event for the three of us to capture together was our church/community-wide fall festival event. A lot of people, locations, and moving parts. Our church had two decent beginner level DSLR (Digital Single Lens Reflex) cameras and I had my own camera. We were set, right?! Throughout the beginning of the event, I watched them both and checked in on them. Every check in time, there was something wrong. Camera battery didn't charge fully, camera wouldn't focus, or they just didn't know how to use the camera.

This was not the interns' fault. It was my fault. I had put equipment in their hands that they (1) did not fully know how to use (2) nor were comfortable using. The little content captured up to that point was unusable for what we needed. So, I did what I should have done in the beginning, I took the cameras out of their hands and said use your iPhone. [Insert gasp.] Yes, I took away the DSLR camera and said take pictures and video on your iPhone instead. Why? Because teenagers know how to use their smartphones and know how to capture great content on their smartphones and know how to be comfortable with that piece of equipment. This made all the difference in the world. From a quality and value perspective, we captured greater content using this equipment because the equipment was known how to be used.

Fast forward two years from that event, these two interns have both taken a great interest in photography, learned how to use professional camera equipment, consistently capture fantastic content for our church events and services, and have both started their own photography businesses. While they have traded in their iPhones for professional cameras and lenses, they first had to learn how to use the equipment to become comfortable and capture valuable content.

Following the church photography example, I recently had someone ask me about how they could improve their church photography and what equipment they needed. My first question to them, "What equipment do you have?" Their response, "Well, I have my iPhone and a camera to use if I need it, but I have no clue how to use the camera." That response did not even require me to ask my second question of what piece of equipment they were more comfortable using. I immediately responded with "use your phone". This person looked at me puzzled, so I shared the intern story with them.

Guess what? People still positively responded on different platforms to both the content shot on the iPhone and on the camera. Why? Because at the end of the day in marketing, the audience does not care what equipment you use. They just want to know what is going on. They just want to see what is happening. The audience is not critiquing the behind the scenes production. Your audience does not want to see a blurred picture from a camera that you do not know how to use. They would rather see the clear picture taken on a smartphone that tells a story. They just want valuable content to consume.

Exercise: How do you determine what equipment is necessary to start with? Write down the platforms you selected in the last exercise. Beside each platform, write down what type of equipment is necessary to produce quality content to each platform. Once that is written down, start your research to determine for each piece of equipment which option gives you the best quality for the lowest price.

For some equipment, will it take some investment? Yes. However, with the availability of consumer-friendly products that are on the market, equipment need not break the bank. The resources are plentiful that help you create and share meaningful content for little cost. Maybe for right now, your universal piece of equipment is your smartphone and your investment is specific apps for content creating. Then down the road you can invest in a computer and learn how to use industry standard graphics software. Only you and your church know what your church can invest in right now.

Don't discredit the equipment you have and that you are comfortable using. Start with what you know and with what you have. Don't let the budget or learning curve stop you. What equipment do you have right now that can get you started? Is there any type of personal investment that you can make right now? What type of investment can your church make in terms of equipment? Could you speak with your pastor or your finance team about this?

Once you choose what equipment will be best to support your platforms selected and message to be communicated, again, don't let the learning curve hinder you. Remember back to the introduction, for much of my early years in the church marketing world, I felt like I was faking it until I made it. Allow me to be honest and critical for a moment. When I look back on early projects I completed, I should have been fired for what some of the finished projects looked like. While my skill level in the equipment I was using was no way near what I am capable of now, I understood that God had gifted me with three things: (1) the opportunity, (2) the right equipment to do the job well and produce quality, and (3) the resources to learn and continue to improve to learn how to use the equipment. Much of my experience and how I got started in this field came from putting in the work to learn by teaching myself until I could get to college to get formal training. If you do not have the formal training, experience, or degree, I understand because I have been in your shoes. However, that's what has led me to this book and the passion to also help, guide, and equip other church marketers like you on how to help your church effectively share their message (their what) and stand out.

I want to encourage you to remember that the greatest piece of equipment you have as a church marketer is the equipment of the Holy Spirit, who is overall worth far more than any other piece of equipment and platform could ever be valued for. Does that mean we sit with no platforms and no equipment? No, because we are called to be good stewards of the resources God has given us and to actively live in the equipment God has given each of us. The writer of Hebrews promises us that God will "equip you with everything good that you may do his will, working in us that which is pleasing in his sight, through Jesus Christ, to whom be glory forever and ever. Amen." (Hebrews 13:21, ESV). As a Christian working for the advancement of His Kingdom, God has chosen you for a specific and special work for His Church and His people. Therefore, He will equip you. I am sure you are familiar with the infamous phrase, "God does not call the equipped; He equips the called." This calling into this field may not make sense for your life and you may feel lost in the 'what', but I promise that if you continue living in what He has called you to He will equip you properly. It will require you to stretch yourself to learn new things and continue to improve no matter what equipment you choose, but in the end it will be worth it.

For now though, do not overwhelm yourself with all the equipment out there. Much like with what platforms to choose, take it one step at a time and prioritize necessary equipment based upon what platforms you have selected, your budget, and also your expertise. Start small but mighty. Remember, with the Holy Spirit in your heart and a smartphone in your pocket, you can be extremely effective.

CHAPTER 6
WHERE? / WHEN?
WHERE ARE THE PEOPLE AND WHEN ARE THEY THERE?

When I receive a graphics/promotional package request, two of the questions I ask are (1) where is it and (2) when is it? The answers to these questions contain vital information because it tells the audience where they are supposed to go and when they are supposed to go there. Moreover, to share the information to your audience you have to share it where the people are and when they are present.

In marketing it is essential that you (1) talk where the people are and (2) talk when the people are present. If you don't, people will never see or hear you. Knowing the when and where of your audience also guides you in what platforms you choose. For example, you may like Facebook, but for your church's student ministry and reaching the next generation, Facebook is not where the students of your church are.

To determine where and when your audience are, go back to the audience identification and segmentation. Proper segmentation of your audience's demographics, psychographics, and geographics will help you determine the when and where your audience will be. Once you know that, you can pinpoint the most effective platforms to be present on for each ministry you are marketing.

As church marketers, we can learn a great deal about the importance of going where the people are and when they are there from the example Jesus left during His earthly ministry. Jesus' earthly ministry consisted of doing ministry where the people were and when they were present.

In nine instances of Jesus' earthly ministry, Jesus initiated conversation with the people. One instance is the woman at the well. When the Samaritan woman came to the well to draw water, Jesus was the first to speak and asked her, "Will you give me a drink?" (John 4:7, NIV). This act of Jesus going to where this woman would be, at the well, and going to the well when she would be there to draw water turned into her not only believing in Him but also in her going back to the town to tell the people to, "come, see a man who told me everything I ever did. Could this be the Messiah?" (John 7:29, NIV).

Going directly where she was, when she was there resulted in her belief and others coming to see Jesus. Go where the people are, when they are there and you will increase your reach.

Another example of Jesus going directly to the people and initiating the conversation was the healing of the crippled man. When Jesus learned of the man's condition, He asked the man, "Do you want to get well?" (John 5:6, NIV). The crippled man replied with, "I have no one to help me into the pool when the water is stirred." (John 5:7, NIV).

This crippled man had no one to help him. Even if this man wanted to go to church, he could not go. Even if he knew Jesus could heal him, he had no way to get to Jesus. Jesus had to come to him. Jesus did just that. He went to where the man was and when he was there.

There are people in the world who are so crippled by sin that they do not even know they need healing, much less know where and when to go to receive healing and salvation.

The Church may be the hospital for the spiritually sick, but we must go directly to where the people are and when they are there in order to let them know we have treatment available and to be able to transport the ones who cannot find their own way to the Church building.

When Jesus fed the 5,000, He and His disciples were sitting on the mountaintop to pray when they saw the people gathering down below. Jesus came down off the mountain to serve the people. He came to where the people were, when they were there in order to serve them and feed them.

Very few of Jesus' conversations took place in a religious setting. Most of His conversations on Earth took place in the workplace or in the home.

When Jesus called James and John to follow Him and be two of His disciples, He did not call them to follow Him in a Sunday service. Jesus went to their workplace. Since they were fishermen, Jesus went to James and John's boat as they were preparing their nets. In the Bible Jesus called them and "immediately they left the boat and their father and followed Him" (Matthew 4:22, NIV).

When Jesus saw Zacchaeus in the sycamore tree, Jesus looked up at him and told him that he had to stay at his house. Zacchaeus went into a state of repentance. Jesus told him that salvation had come to his house. Jesus also said, "For the Son of Man came to seek and to save the lost" (Luke 19:10, NIV).

To seek and to save the lost. Seeking means to go out and find. Are we as the church seeking? Are we as the church going out to find? Seeking involves having to go where these people are, when they are there. It does not mean waiting for them to come to you.

I love Brady Shear's, founder of Pro Church Tools, thoughts on the significance of 167 hours. Church does not just happen on Wednesdays or Sundays. Typically, a Sunday worship service lasts about an hour. That's one hour out of a 24-hour day. That's one hour of 168 total hours in a week. So, how is the church connecting with its people the other 167 hours of the week?

If the Church is a community of believers, then it's a family. Do you only connect with your family for only one hour a week? Probably not. But does that mean you have 100 worship services a week? No, it means your church must find ways to connect with people in the church building, in their schools, in their places of work, in their homes, and on their electronic devices. Where the people are and when they are there.

While we've been talking about how this relates to ministry, how does this all relate to marketing in your church?

Once you've identified who your church's audience is, you then have to set up the event or message you are promoting to actually reach the audience. To reach your church's audience, you have to know where your audience gathers.

Think about where your people are. Where are the places in your community that they gather? For your student ministry and children's ministry, where are the schools the majority of your families are a part of? Where are the neighborhoods where your people live? Are there certain workplaces where your people work? Where are the platforms they are active on?

Overall, where are your people gathering outside of the church building? Where are they living?

Where are your people?

When you are able to answer those questions, then your job as a marketer is to take your church's message there. Take your 'what' to the 'where.'

Remember the 'what.' Remember your church's message.

Remembering your church's 'what' also gives you insight of where to market and when to market. Knowing the specific 'what' allows you to properly determine the exact 'where.' If the 'what' being promoted is a special student ministry event, then the 'where' is probably not going to include Facebook or a senior living center. For this particular student ministry event, the most effective 'where' could include Instagram or at the schools in proximity to your church.

Your specific 'where's' within your marketing plans will be contingent upon your specific 'who's' (audiences).

Now, for more about your 'when'. Knowing who your audience is and where they are also includes knowing the 'when'. The 'when' deals with the timing.

Are there specific events during the year that your audience tends to react more with? For example, Easter and around Christmas are always the two biggest Sundays of the year in the church calendar. It is when the church sees some of its biggest numbers of people. So, think about your timing, your 'when' in the promotion of these dates.

On social media, think about when your people are most active on the platforms you are present on. Are they on Facebook more in the morning or at night? Think about the timing of the posts.

Again, church marketing is not just about connecting with your people on Sundays and Wednesdays. It is not just about marketing to your people to bring them inside the church building.

Think back to what I said earlier about the hours in a day and total hours in the week. People live lives on Monday, Tuesday, Thursday, Friday, and Saturday too. Marketing is not just promoting on these non-church-service days. Your church marketing must involve connecting with the people.

Why? Because church is about doing life together. Humans are naturally designed by God to be relational people. There is no getting around that. Therefore, your marketing has to be relational.

I believe church marketing has to be even more relational because there is no traditional product/service like a ecular organization. Your organization is people. Remember, the church is the community of believers, not the building.

If you go where the people are, when they are there, then you are connecting with their daily lives. Your church is doing life with your people.

Our ability to reach people directly where they are is greater now than ever before. So why don't we go directly where the people are?

If the church does not go directly where the people are, then other organizations and messages will, and I cannot promise that these messages will be Christian and promote the name of Jesus. Therefore, the church must go where the people are.

Meet people where they are and when they are there. Why? Because Jesus did.

With that in mind, let's focus on social media for a moment and allow me to offer further discussion on what social media platforms you should be on. I once heard a discussion about social media platforms and the ones where people needed to be present for marketing purposes where you could gain the most followers.

While I agree with part of that statement, don't just go where you'll get the most likes and followers. Go where your audience is. Go where you'll get the most followers of Christ. Our world has trained us to be focused on getting the most likes and followers. Don't get me wrong, from a marketing standpoint and analytic perspective, you have to be concerned with the likes and followers to an extent to ensure your social media marketing plan is effective.

However, in church marketing, you have to have the humility to see marketing with a ministerial lens to see the number and gain of *followers of Christ* above the number and gain of followers of social media.

With that, it forces you to be sensitive to having to go where and when the people are even if that means stretching you to places and times you did not want to go.

This reminds me of Jonah. God told Jonah to go and He gave Jonah a specific place and time to go. God told Jonah to "Go to the great city of Nineveh and preach against it, because its wickedness has come up before me" (Jonah 1:1).

God had a specific purpose for this place and time, this where and when. Being familiar with the story, you know that Jonah did not want to go to Nineveh and refused to go, so he took matters into his own hands. Jonah went down to Joppa and boarded the ship headed for Tarshish in an attempt to flee from the Lord.

We all know where the story heads from there. God sent the storm, Jonah got thrown overboard, and the big fish swallowed Jonah where he stayed for three days and three nights. God had a specific place and time for Jonah since he did not go to Nineveh.

The problem was not that Jonah did not want to share God's message that God had given him to share. The problem was that Jonah did not want to share God's message where God wanted and called Jonah to share it. Jonah did not want to share 'what' in the 'where' and 'when' and to the 'who' God had called and sent Jonah to.

Once God put Jonah back on dry land, God came to Jonah a second time and told Jonah, "Go to the great city of Nineveh and proclaim to it the message I give you" (Jonah 3:1-2, NIV). With this, "Jonah obeyed the word of the Lord and went to Nineveh" (Jonah 3:3, NIV).

Again, we know how the story goes from there. Jonah's warning from the Lord reached the King. The king issued a decree to the people of Nineveh telling them to turn from their wicked ways, hoping God would spare them. God seeing that the people of Nineveh repented and indeed turned from their evil ways, God showed the people of Nineveh mercy and did not bring upon them his threatened destruction.

Through Jonah's story, we see what disobedience to God brings. We also see what obedience brings. But in relation to this chapter, here's the big point that I don't want us to miss…

Through Jonah's story, we see the powerful impact that is had when we take the 'what' (God's message) to the 'who' God has called us to and sent us to the specific 'where' and 'when.'

In church marketing, you must be sensitive to the 'where' and 'when' of your people and the 'where' and the 'when' of God's calling for your church. The 'where' and 'when' may not be the most popular places to market and communicate. It may not allow you to use the best trends or the most popular ways. However, God has a reason for the 'where' and 'when.'

I once heard someone in the marketing field complaining where God had called them. The complaints consisted of, "If I was somewhere like there, I could do designs like this." "If I was somewhere like there, I could utilize those great resources." "If I was somewhere like over there, I would have a much better social media following and be able to get more likes." "If I was somewhere like there, I could do my marketing job much better." "If I was somewhere like there, I could communicate much better." See a pattern? "If I was somewhere like there…"

While 'somewhere' may seem better, God has placed you in a specific place and for a specific time for a specific people. To reach those people, you must go where the people are, when they are there in order to effectively reach them.

CHAPTER 7
HOW?
HOW DO WE DO IT?

Until this point, we have narrowed down how to identify the who, what, where, when, and why. Once we do all that though, how do we accomplish this? How do we accomplish communicating the mission God has called us to? How do we reach the audience, the group of people God has called us to? How do we actively and effectively reach our people where God has called us and when He has called us? How do we do it? Answering the 'how' can be difficult because I believe this is where we get caught up in ourselves and our lack of abilities and resources. The 'how' is where we can fall into the pitfall of discouragement as church marketers. Knowing who you are as a church, who your audience is, what platforms/equipment to use to reach them at the right place and the right time can build a pep rally. Then when it is time to chart out the action behind our plans and actually do the work, we're halted by the question of how do we do it?

This concept of 'how' is not just in church marketing, as we all want to know how to do things in life. We want to know the process that takes us from point A to point B. With a recipe, the ingredients and the materials can all be listed for you, but they mean nothing without instructions (how). With all of the tutorials and resources out and available, it is clear that there are many people searching for the 'how'. In fact, figuring out how to do this church marketing thing is likely what led you to read this book in the first place. You are a church marketer trying to figure out how to make church marketing simple.

Even in my own experience, I am always the one asking how to do it. I have been known to have a stubborn streak that forces me to not quit until I figure out how to do something well. I'll never forget sitting in a high school math class where I knew without a shadow of a doubt that I would fail the quiz the following day, due to having no clue how to solve the math problems the quiz would cover. Not knowing how was really biting me at this point and I refused to let this one math concept defeat me in a subject I had always succeeded in. As we sat in class working among ourselves to review for the quiz, I took my textbook, notebook, pencil, and calculator, walked to my teacher's desk, placed all of my things on her desk, and pulled a chair to her desk that somewhat blockaded her. Knowing this teacher well enough to be straightforward with her, I looked at her and said, "Look! I don't know how to do this and I refuse to fail this quiz tomorrow, so I'm going to sit here and you're going to show me how to solve this math concept. Even if this bell rings or Jesus Himself returns first, I'm not moving from this seat until I understand how." The teacher responded with a laugh, because of knowing me and then said, "Then let me show you how." Guess what? By the time the bell rang at the end of class, I considered myself an expert on that math concept and aced that quiz the following day. It all happened though because I was willing to ask how and not stop until I understood it.

Because of my curious and inquisitive nature, asking how and wanting to know how have always been priority for me. I not only love asking how and figuring out how though, I also love when people ask me how and getting to teach and show others how to do something.

Call it my inner teacher. How to make church marketing simple and help fellow church marketers is what even led me to write this book. I wanted to show you how in the simplest way possible. I love it when I get to show others how, especially in fields that I am passionate in. Whatever it may be, I not only want to understand the 'how', but I also want to show others how.

The 'how' is not understood until the question is first asked. You have to be willing to learn and understand the process before you can emulate the process, whatever it may be. Whether it's training for sports, learning how to play an instrument, in the marketing sense, learning a new platform or a new piece of equipment even. You have to be willing to ask the questions, put in the work, and have a willingness to learn to figure out the how. Again, it's the how that maps out your process, or your journey, between point A to point B.

In the ever advancing and changing digital world we live in, technology and the best marketing practices are constantly evolving, so you must be prepared to continue to learn how. Learning never stops because the process is always being refined to be more effective. In this one chapter, I could cover stacks of how-to's in church marketing and communications from branding to welcoming guests and still not cover everything.

However, for the purpose of this framework that we're working through in this book, if I had to give you one universal answer to the how to make church marketing simple it's this: be your authentic self. Let your church be authentic. Market your church authentically. Communicate about your church authentically. Be authentic.

People are facing incoming lies from every direction in the world. Fake is a word we attach to multiple sources, to the point where people look like they are watching a tennis match watching the ball go from side to side attempting to figure out which side is telling the truth and which side is lying to them. People are searching for truth. People are searching for authenticity. If people cannot find truth and authenticity in church, then is there anywhere in the world they can find truth and authenticity at this point? A bit of hard truth for a moment, if people wanted to face facades, they could find better and less judgmental places to deal with fakeness than having to deal with it in church. If people are searching for and craving truth and authenticity, then be the church and be who God has called you to be as His body. As a church, if you're asking people to come in and be real, then you have to be real with them first.

Let's picture a house. Your front porch can be decorated to give off an appealing vibe that entices people and seems inviting. However, once a guest is invited inside your house, does the vibe inside the home match what enticed them to step onto the front porch to begin with? Is the inside of the home as inviting as the front porch?

Once inside the home and part of the home, are people going to receive the same vibe coming in and out of the side and back doors as they did when first entered through the front door?

At one of my grandmother's house, no one ever comes through her actual front door. Most people always come through her side door and have done that for the fifty-plus years she has lived in that house. Why? Well, that's the door the family has always gone in. Even after a delivery person has delivered to the front porch once, most delivery people return using the side door only. As I am typing this out, I had to pause and think if I had ever even walked through her front door, and that house is literally my second home. The same concept applied to my great-grandparents house. Once you had entered that house at least once, you no longer entered through the front door, you entered through the back-porch door. However, no matter what door you entered through either house, you were greeted with a true welcome inside the home. If you entered through the actual front door, you weren't greeted with a well-rehearsed greeting and then given a different greeting at the back door. The welcome and vibe matched at either door.

Why is it important that the front porch and the front door match inside your door and at the back door? Because we as humans can put on a good face at the front door. We can do what it takes to make a good first impression. However, once people are inside and get to know you, are they still willing to stay?

I spoke to a couple visiting a church once and the conversation turned to where I asked what led them to search for a new church home. They said that their previous church was a bigger church in the area and from the outside they felt like it was the perfect church for them. It was what they had been searching for, which was a church that offered meaningful small groups, valuable serving opportunities, and a strong student ministry for their child. As they detailed this, I asked them what went wrong. They responded, "From the outside they said all the right things, but once we got on the inside and tried to get connected, it wasn't what it seemed."

"It wasn't what it seemed." That phrase slashed me for three major reasons: (1) I was working in ministry and that is not what you want to hear, (2) I am in marketing and that phrase sounds like a marketing plan gone bad, (3) I knew what it felt like to be in their shoes as a church guest.

At this point in my life, I have been a church guest (or church homeless, you could say) at three points in my life. Each time nothing had gone wrong, it was simply God's direction to lead my family to another place. I am thankful for the three church homes I have had in my life, as each has rallied behind me and played a critical role in my spiritual and discipleship development. So, to anyone who might be reading this that I went to church with, thank you. During those seasons I, along with my family, openly questioned God and now looking back, I see more clearly His reasons. For me personally, I have been able to apply my own church guest experience to my church marketing work as I can see things from the guest perspective. This church guest journey is for an entirely different book (so stay tuned). However, for this chapter, I have visited churches where the front door/front porch did not match the inside. Dare I say the front door was just to entice.

Churches cannot make their front door look like something they are not. You can make the most edge cutting graphics, have the nicest writing pens, the greatest signage, or the trendiest student ministry t-shirt. If it doesn't match who you are as a church, then just stop while you are ahead.

In the digital world we live in, giving off a different persona is more easily done. Social networks have become highlight reels of people's lives and churches are not excluded from that. Digital platforms, such as social networks, are the digital front doors for churches. We live in a world where people are more likely to visit your church website and social networks before they walk onto your campus. More people decide to actually visit your church based on what they see on your church's website and social networks. With that information, platform selection and the when and where becomes even more important to nail as church marketers.

Through social networks and other digital platforms, we could easily hide behind a screen and write a completely different narrative of our church online if we wanted to. Once you got people through the doors of your actual campus though, would your church's voice match the voice people had seen online on social media?

When a new church member was asked what led him to my church, he responded that he and his wife thoroughly searched the church's social media platforms before they ever decided to visit the campus. While they had heard of the church and the great things happening, they wanted to see what its social activity was like. When they scrolled through the church's social platforms, they saw evidence of what they were looking for in a church for their family. Perhaps it was time to actually try to the church and see if what they saw on social was what would be experienced on the actual church music. Much to my relief, he said what they experienced and saw firsthand on campus matched what they saw online. A huge exhale escaped me because those words meant everything. Our voices matched.

People don't want a different voice online than what they experience on campus. People want a consistent authentic voice in every aspect of their church. People respond to authenticity.

There is a myriad of languages spoken across our world, and even within the same languages there are multiple dialects. For me, being born, raised, and living in Georgia, I have a deep southern dialect. That's who I am. When I travel out of state and others hear me speak, I always get, "What part of the south are you from?" Part of my identity is contained in my voice. Being from Georgia is part of who I am, and it influences my voice.

The same goes for your church. God has given you a specific location, a specific purpose, and a specific mission and this influences your voice as a church. Your church's voice is part of your church's identity. Finding your church's voice and speaking in your church's voice all goes back to establishing who you are. God has given your church a specific voice, so don't try to change it. Actively speak in that voice because there are people (your audience) who are actively seeking a group of believers that speak like them. So why would we attempt to market and promote a different voice?

If you are like me, you often follow other churches (usually bigger churches) on social media. I endlessly scroll through other churches' profiles, websites, and graphics. I do it as a source of inspiration and a place of learning. However, I will be the first to admit that it is easy to fall into the comparison trap when doing this.

Exercise: Which comparison traps have you fallen into? Write down any others that I haven't mentioned.

"Oh, their graphics look better!"

"Why can't my church invites look that good?"

"Look at that Guest Services desk!"

"If only I had a marketing budget like that."

"If only the church environment looked like this."

"If only we had this."

"If only we had that."

"If only..."

"If only..."

"If only..."

This comparison trap leads you more into what you wish your church could do compared to what other churches are doing instead of pursuing where you are in the present and where God is leading you. Falling into this comparison trap pushes you into a place of discouragement and stopping. If you can't do what that church is doing, what's the point in doing anything at all? Sound familiar?

I have been there, and I repeatedly fall into the trap. Remember though, we are only human, and we constantly are in the fight against flesh in every aspect of our lives. Does this mean we are not to look to other churches and see what they are doing? No, because we can benefit as churches to learn from each other. At the end of the day, we are all one body of believers all working for the same thing, the advancement of His Kingdom. I urge you to look at other churches for sources of inspiration and ideas.

Don't let this persuade you to be a copycat though. I believe we are living in a time where churches are more concerned in doing things exactly like other churches (more specifically the bigger churches) to try and gain relevance and attract more people. "Because Church A does it like this and they are seeing success, let's try to copy it." Many churches' marketing strategies have become, "Let's do it just like them." With that strategy, you are headed straight for failure.

If God wanted you to be exactly like Church A, then He would have made you Church A. Marketing strategies cannot be copied word for word, tactic for tactic and succeed for everyone. God did not call your church to be a copycat of another local church, so don't market it like one. Quit living in the shadow of the church you wish you could be and live in mission of who He has called your local church to be.

If people wanted to be a part of Church A, then they would go to Church A. Not being a carbon copy of Church A is not what is keeping people from your church. That is a shallow answer that requires you as a church leader and marketer to dive deeper into who you are and who your audience is to discover where the two converge.

I'll say it again, people desire authenticity. People want to see your flaws, blemishes, and scars, because they themselves are flawed, blemished, and scarred. People crave to see the realness rather than a perfectly packaged product placed on a pedestal that they feel they have to live up to.

While people may have to shield these portrayal betrayals, that does not give a license for you as a church marketer to do the same. There is no need to give off a false portrayal. The Gospel is just as it seems. There is no need for a 100% money back guarantee disclaimer, because the Gospel has a 100% satisfaction rate guaranteed. With that, there is no reason for us as marketers to be anything but real and authentic.

People hunger and thirst for authenticity now more than ever. According to a recent consumer survey by Stackla, research found that nearly ninety percent of consumers say that authenticity is a key factor to decide the brands they support. With that high of a percentage of people craving authenticity, then churches are at an advantage because churches have the Truth. There is nothing more authentic and absolute than God and the Gospel.

As people crave authenticity, Jesus also desires our authenticity. Why? Because He has given us our voice and identity to begin with. In giving His model on how to pray in the Sermon on the Mount, Jesus warns that, "when you pray, do not be like the hypocrites, for they love to pray standing in the synagogues and on the street corners to be seen by others. Truly I tell you, they have received their reward in full." (Matthew 6:5, NIV). When you speak, don't be hypocritical. Be authentic.

In his letter to the Corinthians, Paul writes, "Now this is our boast: Our conscience testifies that we have conducted ourselves in the world, and especially in our relations with you, with integrity and godly sincerity. We have done so, relying not on worldly wisdom but on

God's grace" (1 Corinthians 1:12, NIV).

It's easy to conform in the world and change your message and voice for the sake of relevance. However, we must conduct ourselves in an authentic manner with integrity and godly sincerity, relying on God. When we speak in this authentic voice and posture, then we are marketing and communicating an absolute Truth that the world can in no way match.

Paul tells the Philippians that he "eagerly [expects] and [hopes] that I [Paul] will in no way be ashamed but will have sufficient courage so that now as always Christ will be exalted in my body, whether by life or by death" (Philippians 1:20, NIV). We should in no way be ashamed of the voice that God has given us as a church and should instead go out with boldness that Christ may be magnified within us as a body of believers so that the world sees Christ exalted and glorified through it all.

While there are many more specific how-to's in the church marketing world, the universal 'how' to accomplish first is to be your authentic self. If you want to make church marketing simple, how do you do it? Be your authentic self.

CHAPTER 8
HOW?
HOW DO I PLAN?

We can talk about selecting what platforms, what equipment, being equipped by God, and also how to be yourself in church marketing. All of that can seem overwhelming if you are trying to juggle it all without a plan.

I do not think the question to ask is whether or not you should plan in church marketing. Rather, the question should be *how* do I plan in church marketing.

I say there are two types of people: there are the planners and there are those who fly by the seat of their pants. Sometimes you might get fortunate enough to get a true blend of the two.

Personally, I am a planner through and through. I am a Type A person. If you are into Enneagrams, I am nearly an equal one and three. I love plans. I love lists. If you are talking to me, you will even find I often talk in lists. Planning things is in my nature. It's in my nurture. It's part of who I am. That's not going to change.

Being in the marketing and communications fields, my love of planning and personality have served me well. When I had to do my first full official marketing plan for one of my college courses, I will admit that I was overwhelmed because it was a daunting task. However, it became easier each time I did it.

Like I said, planning is essential in church marketing because any type of marketing needs a plan. It just makes all things marketing easier when you have a plan to connect to and refer to. If you don't have that plan, you can easily get lost and lose sight of what the intended goal for your marketing campaign was in the first place. While I do believe that marketing requires a plan, it does not have to be not be elaborate or eloquent.

Write your social media posts in the notes app on your phone. Write down your weekly tasks with pen and paper, even a sticky note will do the trick. Type plans out on a document. Use an app to organize everything.

How you plan need not be fancy. Just use the systems you are most comfortable with to organize your church marketing plan.

In business plans and in marketing plans, your organization's goals, systems, strategies, processes, and more are detailed and discussed. However, these systems, strategies, and processes do not just occur in the secular world with large corporations. These occur in the church world too, whether we realize or not and whether or not we attach those actual names to it.

I have heard stories of pastors who are against planning because they believe you just need to trust God. Planning, in this case marketing plans, are not needed in the church because God does not operate on business plans or marketing plans.

While that is true and I fully believe that God's plans are much higher and better than a business plan, understand that when I say planning I'm not saying to create a marketing plan to submit to God for review.

Seek the Lord for His plan and His purpose, and then plan accordingly in His direction. Planning does not eliminate God's purpose and vision. Instead, planning helps form the steps toward accomplishing His purpose and vision.

Planning as a church team and in church marketing can help your ministries be more effective as you, your church, and your church's leadership can get aligned.

For marketing and communications purposes specifically, let's take Vacation Bible School (VBS) as an example in your children's ministry. If your church has VBS or something similar every summer, you know that it is one of the greatest and largest evangelism events that your church probably puts on every year. Not only are your church kids coming but you are also bringing in numerous children from the community. It requires a great deal of volunteers, including those that never serve in children's ministry regularly. This event takes the entire church to come together and reaches into the entire community.

This event especially takes special planning. Planning for teaching, planning for the actual events, planning for the schedule, planning for volunteers, planning for promotion. It takes a lot of sectors for it to come together seamlessly, or as seamlessly as possible to the eyes of a child, for the children that week.

I see the necessity of planning for an event like this from multiple perspectives. I see it from the volunteer perspective as I have volunteered in countless weeks of VBS. I see it from the perspective of the child of a Children's Director. (My mom coordinated many VBSs during her time as a Children's Director. That's a whole new level of planning right there. Shout out to the Children's Directors of churches! We love you!) I see it from the perspective of a church marketer.

VBS already brings enough chaos with it naturally. We need not add to it with our lack of planning. The reason I share this example is that planning in an event like this brings alignment to the team and to the event.

I remember my mom would hold a VBS volunteer meeting weeks before the event once she had recruited and placed all of her volunteers. This meeting was to pass out schedules, procedures, rules, and to discuss the entire event. It was to lay the plans for the event out. Doing that got everyone on the same page. It meant that you did not have four classes going to the same craft rotation all at once. It meant that everyone was aligned and knew what to do for this event. Planning made it possible for the event to run with minimal distractions, letting the focus be where it needed to be: on God.

Planning does not go against God's vision and purpose unless we allow it to. In church marketing and in all things, we must be sensitive to His greater plan and purpose and seek His face as we make our own plans.

Planning is not just secular but there is a spiritual aspect of it. God plans and He wants us to plan too and follow plans. Planning can be spiritual if we seek God.

We see the purpose of planning in the Bible. God sent plans to Noah on how to build the ark. The ark was built by Noah following those specific instructions on how to build it. God told Noah **who** it was to be built for, **what** needed to be built, **where** the ark would go, an estimated **when, why** the ark needed to be built, and **how** the ark was to be built.

God had a plan to destroy every living thing on Earth through the flood and had a plan for who He would spare. He had a plan for how He would spare Noah's family, and for the animals too. He had a very specific plan to build the ark. God told Noah to "Make yourself an ark of gopher wood. Make rooms in the ark and cover it inside and out with pitch. This is how you are to make it: the length of the ark 300 cubits, its breadth 50 cubits, and its height 30 cubits. Make a roof for the ark, and finish it to a cubit above, and set the door of the ark in its side. Make it with lower, second, and third decks" (Genesis 6:14-16, ESV).

Furthermore, God told Noah "you shall come into the ark, you, your sons, your wife, and your sons' wives with you. And of every living thing of all flesh, you shall bring two of every sort into the ark to keep them alive with you. They shall be male and female. Of the birds according to their kinds, and of the animals according to their kinds, of every creeping thing of the ground, according to its kind, two of every sort shall come into you to keep them alive. Also take with you every sort of food that is eaten and store it up. It shall serve as food for you and for them" (Genesis 6:18-21, ESV).

What I love though is verse 22 in this chapter, "Noah did this; he did all that God commanded him" (Genesis 6:22, ESV). Noah followed the plans of God. He followed the 'how' and Noah and his family saw the blessing from it.

There is beauty and fruit that comes from the labor of planning when we follow God's calling.

When He was telling the large crowds about the cost of being a disciple and having to be willing to give up everything, Jesus' examples also provide insight to the importance of planning.

Jesus said, "Suppose one of you wants to build a tower. Won't you first sit down and estimate the cost to see if you have enough money to complete it? For if you lay the foundation and are not able to finish it, everyone who sees it will ridicule you, saying, 'This person began to build and wasn't able to finish'" (Luke 14:28-30, NIV).

In planning, in church marketing, in determining our 'how,' are we willing to count the cost? In church marketing, we can relate to this parable in the literal sense. Whether you have an extensive budget or no budget, you have to count the cost to see you if you have enough money to complete it. If we lay the foundation for a church marketing plan and cannot finish it, people will see this.

Now let me be clear: I'm not saying that our end goal as church marketers is to be people pleasers and do things solely to avoid ridicule, because be ready to receive both positive and negative feedback. What I am saying is to count the cost of your 'how'. What is it going to take in your church marketing? What's the plan? What's the cost of the plan? You have to be prepared.

What are the financial costs of your plans, your 'how', going to be? What are the creative costs of your plans, your 'how', going to be? What are the time costs of your plans, your 'how', going to be?

What are the overall costs of your 'how'? This is another reason why planning is essential. Counting the costs. Truly planning. Not forgetting to determine the 'how' in your 'who, what, where, when, and why' can help eliminate the feeling of being overwhelmed for you.

Remember, God even had a plan for redemption through Jesus. God had a 'who, what, where, when, and why' for redemption, but His 'how' was the plan of fulfillment, from Jesus and His birth to His crucifixion to His resurrection to His ascension to His second coming.

Here are verses about planning that we can apply to our lives as church marketers:

> "Many are the plans in a person's heart, but it is the Lord's purpose that prevails." (Proverbs 19:21 NIV)

> "In their hearts humans plan their course, but the Lord establishes their steps." (Proverbs 16:9 NIV)

One verse we need to cling to in planning out the specific 'how' for our church marketing plans is, "Plans fail for lack of counsel but with many advisers they succeed." (Proverbs 15:22 NIV).

In your planning, seek advice and counsel in an effort to see success. You do not have all the answers. Be willing to put your pride aside and seek input from others. Even if it is for a graphic or the wording of an email. Remember, while you may be a team of one on the church marketing team, it is not solely your church. It is His Church made up of His people. From the smallest to the biggest of plans, seek advice and counsel for the preparation of success for your marketing plans.

Now that we've been discussing the importance of planning and how to plan, I suspect and hope that your brain has been spinning with ideas, plans, and how-to's for your church marketing plan. However, I now interrupt your thought processes to warn you not to over-plan.

When you over-plan, I believe you become resistant to changes that may come your way. To have to pivot and change would mean to add on new work. Those plans you made did not just happen either, they were plans you had invested time in. Picture it being like finally getting a full place setting ready at a fine dining restaurant and someone coming along and ripping the tablecloth out from under it. It doesn't feel good.

With me being a planner, I like to plan ahead, and I'll admit that I do not like when plans change, especially all of the sudden. However, in my life, I feel like that is where God always tugs at me by halting me in my tracks and changing my course to His destination.

My family and I love to go to Disney World and frequently visit there throughout the year. As often as we have gone, we have the path there and back down to an art. If we leave at a specific time early in the morning, then we know the exact time we are going to cross onto Disney property. Coming home it is an identical routine. We know our time to leave to beat Florida traffic then to beat Georgia traffic. If we're off by even thirty minutes, it can change our entire plan. Our travel plan is traffic-proof, or so we thought.

We had traveled down to Disney World for spring break and were not returning until that Sunday, the final day of spring break. We knew what time we had to be in the car early that morning and we would be due back home early afternoon with plenty of time to unpack when we got home and get ready for school the next day.

All was going according to plan until we hit traffic and came to a screeching halt. For the next two hours, we barely moved. It was literally a stop and go situation. Some people even turned off their ignitions around us. The traffic jam then put us in rush hour traffic in another part of Florida, which pushed us even further off our plan. Then we were thrust into Georgia traffic that was a melting pot of spring break travelers congregating on one interstate. At that point, the quickest, yet no so quick, route was to detour and take the backroads. That long journey home turned a 7.5-hour trip into a 13-

hour trip.

We were exhausted when we pulled into the garage late at night, but I was also thankful for the beauty that we saw on those backroads. It was beauty that would not have been seen if our direction had not been changed. Changing directions and plans can seem inconvenient in the moment but do not miss out on seeing the beauty in the new sights to see on the new path.

You may be like me with it all planned out. You have the itinerary of your marketing plan nailed down or your social media posts written and scheduled for the next month, okay, maybe not month but maybe for the week. You have the interstate exit numbers memorized and even know how many stops you will take. Then God says, "not so fast", leading you to take the scenic route on the country backroads.

Whether you are like that or the complete opposite, hear me when I say there is power in planning, but do not become married to every plan. In marketing, more specifically church marketing, I believe it is easy to get caught up in the routine of the plan. If you know the 'who,' 'what,' 'when,' 'where,' and 'why,' won't the 'how' always look the same? Nope!

To be transparent, I have fallen in that hole of believing that if I could work through the trenches on certain projects, eventually I could get my work to a cookie-cutter situation where I did not have to worry about it as much, that is until God literally pulled the rug out from under me (and the entire world and church world for that matter).

Friday, March 13, 2020 will always be a date that is forever ingrained in me. It marked the beginning of the new normal here in Georgia and much of the nation and world as the coronavirus shadow began to spread and envelop us. As I am writing this, we are still wading through these uncharted waters as a world and as a church with restrictions only beginning to ease. This chapter is being written in real time.

On that fateful Friday, I remember having to go meet with the pastor of the church where I work as Director of Marketing & Communications. Decisions were being made as to whether or not we would have an in-person service that Sunday. How would we communicate this to our people and community? Plans drastically changed that day. As I walked into the church building that Sunday, it was only the staff, production team, and worship team there as we streamed the service live. It was literally like living in a twilight zone.

That next day I remember sitting in my office, ready to make out my weekly lists of tasks and upcoming projects. As I started writing, I had to stop myself because everything on that list would have to be done differently or cancelled altogether.

I crumpled up that paper of my well-thought out 'how' and the tears poured down my face in my office with reality sinking in that church was no longer the same and the marketing plan, the church plan even, had made a complete transformation practically overnight. It was literally living out the saying, "out with the old and in with the new."

When I got home that evening, I cried some more and I eventually mustered up the words to cry out, "God, You're going to have to show me *how* to do this now." The problem was that as a person I was allowing my flesh to blur my vision, causing me not to see as clearly as a marketer and communicator. To plow forward through a pandemic in my role and areas, I had to keep my eyes clear and wide open to the un-walked path set before us.

Why? Because churches have to remain resolute. We have to

show faith over fear. We have to show strength over trembling. If trusting God is what we have always proclaimed and promoted, then a pandemic is a moment of now or never for the Church to communicate that.

From a marketing and communications perspective, this pandemic was a moment marker of where the Church had to show their congregation, community, and the world they would walk the walk and talk the talk. In moments of tragedy, the world, no matter how secular it is, always looks to churches for some sort of comfort. It seems like disasters bring out the inner child in people and those inner children are searching for someone that will hug them to make them feel better, or in the case of COVID-19, socially distant hugs to make them feel better. Moments of tragedy fall to the churches.

But how do you do it? This was not taught in marketing classes. This was not taught in communications classes. This was not taught in seminary. Facing a pandemic was not taught anywhere unless you're in the medical field, and even then, I don't believe it went into full detail how to quickly overcome COVID-19.

As I lay in my bed sleepless that Monday night wondering how to navigate this, how to communicate to people, how to reach people, how to plan, how to even live through this, it was like God thumped me on the head. I was too busy focusing on what had changed.

While it's important to consider the changing variables, in marketing you also have to remain focused on what your organization can control. Remember the SWOT analysis from Chapter 2. Opportunities and threats may be external factors that are often uncontrollable, but strengths and weaknesses are internal factors that are controllable.

Yes, the pandemic was a major threat to the church. At the moment of writing this, it still is. However, there remains an opportunity. The choice has to be made whether to allow the uncontrollable to paralyze us or the controllable to push us forward into the new way of church.

It was on that sleepless Monday night that I had to deny my flesh to dwell on the things that had changed and instead concentrate on what had not changed. For our church in the middle of a pandemic who we are did not change, who we reached generally did not change, and what we shared, the Gospel, did not change. The 'where' and 'when' were subject to pivot but did not change dramatically. The platforms we were on changed, but only insofar as the in-person platforms were eliminated and translated to digital platforms we were already a part of. Moreover, our 'why' had not changed. The aspect that did change was our 'how.'

The 'how' may have changed but God has not, nor will He ever. That simple phrase is powerful. Pandemic or not, that phrase should motivate you in church marketing. Your 'how' will change, but God is unchanging.

Realizing and accepting our church's 'how' changing saw our live stream services reach people in Croatia, Connecticut, Oklahoma, California, Florida, South Carolina, North Carolina, Virginia, Tennessee, and more locations that we never could have reached in our normal in-person services in North Georgia. We even saw salvations happen, despite having only online services. How we had a worship service looked different, but the message shared did not change and it only increased our reach.

In a formal marketing plan, your strategies and tactics are your 'how'. They are how you work toward accomplishing your organizational goals and, ultimately, your organizational mission and vision. Let me put it this way. Your plans. Your platforms. Your tactics may change. Your methods may change, but the message does not change. In the church world, we must utilize ever-changing methods for an unchanging message!

That's worth repeating for you as a church marketer and church leader, so mark it, highlight, do what you have to do to remember this:

In the church world, we must utilize ever-changing methods for an unchanging message!

In being submissive to changing our methods for an unchanging message, I think of Paul. In the New Testament, scholars agree that Paul's letters account for thirteen books of the New Testament. Of these letters, four of Paul's letters were written in prison.

As Paul found himself in prison, he was not exempt from the calling God had given him. While Paul was in isolation from others, that did not exempt Paul from sharing the Gospel, nor did Paul being in prison change the Gospel message. However, it did change how he reached his audiences.

Paul though changed his 'how' in order to reach others with the unchanging Gospel message. Not only did Paul's prison letters, in addition to all of his letters, reach the intended audiences, but they also have reached millions upon millions of people. His words have even reached you and me, and Paul did not even know us.

When we realize that our methods may have to change for an unchanging message and live in that obedience, the reach of the Gospel is limitless.

While I pray and hope plans never have to change in church to the extreme they have had to change to amid the coronavirus pandemic, you, as a church marketer, must be willing and able to pivot your plans.

Exercise: What impact has the pandemic had on your life? The way you plan things, the way your days are spent, the ways you interact with your church? What lessons can you learn from this extraordinary experience, and carry forward in service of your church and community after this? Write these down.

One of my favorite quotes regarding planning comes from Winston Churchill, "Plans are of little importance, but planning is essential." This quote comes in different variations from other world leaders such as former U.S. President Dwight D. Eisenhower and former U.S. President Richard Nixon.

No matter what variation of the quote you use, read, or hear, what is important is to remember that plans will change and even fail sometimes, but that does not remove the necessity of planning. Planning motivates. It aligns. It organizes. It puts the light at the end of the tunnel.

If you look at the words 'how' and 'who,' you will notice they are spelled with the same three letters just in a different variation. So, remember it like this, your 'how' will change to effectively reach your 'who.' Your 'who' will help determine your 'how.'

Remember, as a church marketer, to plan your 'how' but be willing to change as time carries and the environment evolves.

CHAPTER 9
WHY?
WHY DOES YOUR CHURCH EXIST?

Behind everything we do, a specific motivation forces or drives us to accomplish it. Think about it. Why do we brush our teeth every day? To keep from cavities. Why do we have to eat food and drink water? To live. Why do we drive? To get to different locations. Why do we buy a house? To have a place to live.

From the smallest tasks to the biggest decisions in our lives, there is a distinguishable motivation we can identify with. A motivation that drives us to keep pushing and to keep fighting toward the finish line, even when times get difficult. Through the motivation, there is purpose. It all goes back to answering the 'why'. Answering and identifying why we do what we do keeps us focused on the goal, mission, and vision we are working toward despite the obstacles we might face.

The 'why' is the center of an organization. It defines the reason the organization exists. In the case of church marketing, being able to identify and know your church's why goes back to the who you are. Why does your local church exist? If marketers do not have a reason for why they are marketing a specific product, service, or brand, then what is the purpose in marketing?

Clearly knowing and remembering your 'why' guides you in helping make marketing, specifically in this case church marketing, simple because you are now marketing with a purpose.

A great book I recommend to help you with your 'why' and the reason knowing your 'why' is so important is Simon Sinek's book "Start with Why." Seriously, go buy it and read it. In his book, he shares examples of some of the most influential brands and companies we know that start with their 'why'. One of these companies is Apple. In Apple's message to the world of who they are as a company and what they do, they always begin with their 'why'. By beginning with their 'why,' they attract consumers that believe similarly. One of my favorite quotes from Simon is this: "People don't buy WHAT you do, they buy WHY you do it." Say it louder for the people in the back, Simon!

When we put this at the forefront of our minds as marketers, especially church marketers, this changes everything. It changes how we communicate, how we promote, and even how we deal with being overwhelmed. With this mentality of 'why', we are now no longer communicating from the what we are doing perspective, we are now communicating from the why we are doing it perspective. With this mentality of 'why', we are now no longer promoting what we are doing but we are now promoting why we are doing it. With this mentality of 'why', I truly believe it helps diminish the overall feeling of being overwhelmed. The sense of being overwhelmed occurs, at least in my experience, when we get caught up in the 'what'. The craziness and the madness that the details of the 'what' can cause the 'why' to become blurred. When the 'why' is the primary focus, it motivates us to work through the hairiness that the 'what' may cause.

Churches have the greatest 'why' that exists. It is not a product or service to be sold to a consumer. It is not an emotional inspiration and hope that we're persuading others to buy into for a monthly subscription. The Church's 'why' is the only 'why' in existence that is fulfilled with an eternal hope. People are more likely to buy based on feeling rather than full-on rationality. They want to know from marketers how they can feel connected to a product or a service they are contemplating purchasing. For the Church, this is simply because this gift, salvation, that the Church ultimately promotes offers a full-on, eternal connection with a risen Savior who has come to redeem and restore us all for those that believe.

For us, as church marketers, remember that our 'why' includes who you are for and what you are about. Simply having an event and promoting it in the all right ways with the result of a good turn out and a good compliment on the way out the door is positive, but is that accomplishing your why? Is that accomplishing why your ministry exists? How does that event you are promoting tie back to your church's 'why'?

It's often easier to get the specifics on who the event is for, what the event is, where the event is, when the event is, and how the event will go and how they need it promoted, but I always love to hear the 'why' response. I have stumped people before when I ask, "Why are you having this event?" One time I had a response of, "What do you mean why am I doing this? Because I want to." Not a good answer to 'why.' Once I sit down and explain to people why the 'why' is important, it is enlightening to see the light-bulb moment.

Like I said before, people want to know from marketers how they can feel connected to a product or a service they are contemplating purchasing. Your audience wants to be connected to you. As they should, because the Church is not a building, it's a body of believers. The Church is the people. People should be connected. People desire to know your church's 'why' because it becomes a part of their own 'why'.

Your role as a church marketer is not just promo, promo, promo. It's about connecting people in the ministry. It's helping build the bridge between your audience and what you are doing. The bridge is your church's 'why'. The 'why' is the bridge between the 'who' and the 'what'. It is essential to communicate the 'why' behind the 'what.' The 'why' brings purpose to your 'what', no matter the 'what'. Communicating the 'why' behind your church's 'what' creates buy-in. Don't tell people in your church what they should do, tell them why they should do it. Sharing the why connects them and makes them a part of the story.

One of the greatest personal examples I saw this with and had the opportunity to work on developing a promotional plan was a student ministry summer camp. For this camp, the student ministry needed camp scholarships to be able to give to students who, without a scholarship, could not afford to go to summer camp. To raise the scholarships, we needed the help of the people in the church. The platforms we chose to promote the need of scholarships were on our main social networks (Facebook and Instagram), on stage announcements, and targeted churchwide emails. Garnering the attention of people took focusing on raising the scholarships leading from the 'why perspective' rather than leading from the 'what perspective.' Here's the example:

Leading from the 'what perspective' --
Our students are going to summer camp this summer and we need scholarship money for students that cannot afford to go.

Leading from the 'why perspective' --
As we prepare for Student Summer Camp, we are expectant for what God will

do in the lives of our students and we believe that God will change lives at this camp. We have an opportunity for you to invest in the lives of our teenagers and student ministry by sponsoring students to go to summer camp this year. We need your partnership because there are students who will not be able to go and hear the Gospel without your support. If you would like to contribute to our student sponsorships for summer camp, there are several ways to sponsor a student for camp.

Leading from the 'what perspective' just tells what the event is and what we need, money. While the 'what' is detailed in the 'why perspective', leading with the 'why' tells that it's more than just a camp, it's more than just financial support. It's a ministry event where life change will happen. The financial support is an investment in a student's eternity.

Leading with the 'why' shows people how they can be actually part of something rather than just looking from the outside in. In this student camp scholarship promotion, we saw an outpouring of generosity from church members. The ultimate reward we saw with gaining the financial support of church members is that several of the students who were able to go to summer camp only because of a scholarship were saved that week during camp. There were church members that literally invested in a student's eternity.

Know your church's 'why' and lead with your church's 'why'. It transforms your marketing from only promoting, promoting, promoting to marketing with a purpose that is connecting and motivating your church.

Sharing and communicating your 'why' to others tells people, your audience, why they should connect with you. Marketing is the journey in which you are telling your audience why they should buy-in to what you are offering. Only viewing marketing as promo, promo, promo is only skimming the surface of marketing. Marketing requires you to dive deep and to uncover the 'why'. That's what people desire to know ultimately: Why should this matter to them?

Again, lead from the 'why perspective' in your marketing instead of leading from the 'what perspective'. While I shared the Apple example moments ago, the greatest example for us to follow is from Jesus Himself. In Jesus' earthly ministry, He led from His 'why perspective' instead of a 'what perspective'. Yes, Jesus performed many miracles during His time on Earth, and, yes, that did show who He was and give credit to why He was here on Earth. Jesus, however, was very clear to point out His 'why' and the specificity of His 'why'. The miracles were only His 'what', but it was His 'why' that kept Him going all the way until the resurrection.

When Mary, His own mother, asked Him to fix the wine situation at the wedding in Cana, Jesus' response was that His hour had not yet come (John 2:4). Yes, He turned water into wine, but that was not His purpose in coming. That was a 'what'. That was not His 'why'.

As Jesus appeared before Pilate in His journey to the cross and Pilate questioned Jesus' kingship, Jesus responded to Pilate saying, "You say that I am a king. In fact, the reason I was born and came into the world is to testify to the truth. Everyone on the side of truth listens to me" (John 18:37, NIV). He openly declares the reason He came. It was this reason that kept Him on the path toward the cross.

Leading from this 'why perspective', the reason He was born, influenced a great amount of 'what's' in His thirty-three years on Earth. His 'why' influenced the specific 'what' moments. The 'what's' led to many people's temporary healing or satisfaction. The blind man could see, the wedding guests had more wine to drink, the five thousand were fed for one meal. However, what Jesus did allowed for the opportunity to show Himself and the reason He was here. His purpose was exalted in the moment.

Churches do a lot of good within their church walls and outside of the church walls. Even in a lost and dying world, the secular world still expects churches to do good and be charitable within the community. While your church can have the best events and you can promote the pants off of something, if it is only promoting your 'what', it's temporary. Leading from the 'why' gives marketing purpose. Leading from the 'why' exalts your purpose, to see people to come to know Jesus.

The Church's purpose, the Church's 'why', is more than just to be a charity. It's to lead people to Jesus. To make Jesus renown. Lead with that. Market that. Share that. Promote that.

Psalms 96:3 says, "Declare his glory among the nations, his marvelous works among all the peoples!" In this context, the word 'declare' in the Old Testament's original Hebrew form translates to 'saphar'. The word 'saphar' is defined as to count, recount, or relate. Within the Psalms context, 'declare' specifically means to recount. To recount something means to tell someone about something. While Psalms 96:3 is one of these Bible verses that is easy to interpret and understand, breaking this verse down even more explicitly tells us what we should do. Tell someone about God's glory across the world; tell about God's marvelous works among everybody in the world!

You don't have to search hard within the Bible to become clear on what Scripture says about communicating and sharing. I could give you a whole page of nothing but Scripture references that tell us as Christians and as churches to go tell and share. The point in this though is to remember why your church is doing something. Why does your church share? Why does your church exist?

The inquisitiveness of a child is unparalleled. Everything that happens or when they are asked to do something is rebutted with the sharp one-worded answer, "Why?" I was the curious child and was known to always ask the 'why' question. My parents' infamous response typically sounded like, "Because I said so." Sound familiar? When that phrase came out, that sent me into a relentless, broken-record-player type response of "But why?" My parents' response of "Because I said so" was, in my mind, not good enough for me at the moment.

When consumers face the option as to why they should buy a product or service, the company telling the consumer, "because we said so" is not the best answer that leads to the best results for the company. Again, people desire to know the actual 'why'. In reality, people have not changed as much from their childhood as we might think. At the core, we still want to know why.

A man once came to the church office I was working in asking for details about our church. He and his family were new to the area and they were searching for a new church home. That day he had been traveling to churches across the community asking for specific information about each church. Call it being at the right place at the right time, but somehow I became the one answering this man's questions as another staff member gathered printed church materials to give him. While I was putting on the good front on the outside, I was praying on the inside, "Please, Lord, give me the answers," because I had no clue what this man would ask.

He began his questioning with the basics: When are your services, where are your services, what are they like, how should I come dressed? Easy, right? This was simple church information to give. This was like Church Inviting 101. I rattled off those answers and even threw in where he could find all of the information, if he needed it, on the website. The printed materials he was given even reiterated most of the information I just shared with him. Then he took his questioning a step further.

"What do you believe?" While this is a deeper question and requires more thought than just telling a worship service time, still, this is a relatively simple question. In fact, as Christians, we should be always prepared to answer this question. Peter tells us to "always [be] prepared to make a defense to anyone who asks you for a reason for the hope that is in you; yet do it with gentleness and respect." (1 Peter 3:15, ESV). As I shared our basic beliefs, he dove deeper into his questions about our doctrine and specific beliefs. Still we were on the right track of answering these questions, or at least I think we were.

As I was able to give an answer to his every question about what our beliefs are as a church, he then hit with the big question: "Why do you believe what you believe?" There it was, that question of 'why'. Again, my outside appearance was to keep composure as much as possible, but I imagined the inside of my brain going into mass chaos with flashing red lights and alarms going off and file cabinets being flung open trying to form an answer as quick as possible. Thanks to God and only Him, was I able to give what I believe was a solid response.

When I finished my response, he simply said, "Thank you." He then continued and set in to tell us about his earlier church-searching adventures from that day. He said that with several churches, he didn't even get past discovering what the basic details of the church were.

Side note: At least know what time your church services are and what a person can expect to experience during a typical service.

With other churches, he got the basic details, but it all fell apart when he asked what they believed. Again, "always be prepared to give an answer to everyone who asks you to give the reason for the hope that you have" (1 Peter 3:15, NIV). Please know the basics of your church's beliefs and doctrines. If you cannot give an account and explain them, then how do you expect the members of your church to go out into the world and share what they believe? You don't have to give the most-theological sounding answer about your church's beliefs and doctrines, but please know the basics.

Then he shared with us about a church that was able to answer all the basic questions and even described what they believed, but it all went south when they had to detail why. In the attempt to discuss the 'why', the church's beliefs then became misconstrued. This man had no intentions of visiting that church because of their inability to answer the 'why'.

Churches often get asked questions from church members within and also from the world on the outside. Getting asked questions from every direction can be intimidating, overwhelming, and stressful. However, every answer has to be linked back to your church's 'why'. Again, people desire to know the 'why'. Knowing the 'why' and sharing the 'why' invites people into purpose. It allows them to be a part. At the core, people are compelled to be connected to a purpose, to grow in that purpose, and to make a difference with that purpose. They have to know what that purpose is first though. People in your church are looking for the church to help them find their purpose. They are looking for that purpose to connect to. When you share your church's 'why', they attach themselves to that. People are more concerned with why you are doing something than with what you are doing, so share why then.

It's about sharing what Jesus can do for people. Market with a purpose. Knowing your why helps give a clear light at the end of the tunnel and lights the path as the steps are established in how to get to that goal. Clearly knowing and understanding your church's 'why' supports who you are as a church, what you are doing, your where and when, and how you will do it.

In planning events, in promoting church services, in writing social media posts, in selecting platforms to share on, in picking places to share, in designing graphics, in writing emails, or whatever it may be in your daily walk as a church marketer, be able to link everything back to your church's 'why'. If it is not first linked back to your church's 'why', then you cannot lead from the 'why perspective' and you risk getting caught up and overwhelmed by all the details of the 'what's'. Always linking it back to the 'why' ensures that you are capturing the essence of who you are as a church, your mission as a church, and capturing your church's identified targeted audience.

Go out and declare your 'why'. That is marketing with a purpose. You, as a church marketer, have the greatest 'why' to declare. Literally your role is to market the greatest purpose there has ever been, ever was, and ever will be--to make the name of Jesus known. Linking it back to the 'why' gives purpose to the 'what' and the 'how'. Unfortunately, in the marketing world, marketers tend to rely too heavily on the company's 'what' and 'how'. However, the most influential brands and their loyal fan bases show us that consumers are driven and compelled by the 'why'. Don't let your church's marketing rely too heavily on what you do as a church and how you do it, focus on what you do and why you do it. That's church marketing made simple, and more importantly, that is church marketing with a purpose.

CHAPTER 10
WHY?
WHY DO YOU SHARE?

While we have focused on the importance of knowing and sharing your church's 'why', it is essential that we focus on the personal 'why' as well. Why do you do what you do? Maybe you were thrown into the church marketing world. Maybe you are a pastor who has had to also wear the church marketing hat as well. Maybe you are the volunteer that saw a need in your church. The possibilities of how you ended up in this church marketing role are endless, but regardless, you have been called by God into this position for a reason. There is a reason for why you do what you do. A purpose that keeps you motivated and moving forward.

For any job, there is a reason that motivates us to do the job and to do the job well. Ministry is no different. In fact, I believe ministry work requires a greater dedication to remember your 'why' and lead from the 'why perspective', because ministry is hard, and ministry is messy.

The sense of being overwhelmed occurs as the church events pile up and the demands from platforms and people continue to rise. Ministry workers (pastors, staff, and volunteers) can find it easy to throw in the towel. Some days it might be easier to quit the whole church marketing and ministry thing and actually go work in the marketing department for an actual towel company. But we don't. Why? Because we are compelled to communicate.

When I started as an intern, I had to defend my decision of doing what I did at a church many times. People wanted to know why I, Madisen, would intern at a church to learn graphic design and marketing. There were so many other businesses I could go to where I would probably learn more that would potentially lead to more. While that may have been true, I explained that I felt this calling that I had to do it. Once I explained my 'why' and then explained the projects I got to work on, people became intrigued. To take it a step further, most did not even realize the necessity of marketing and communications in churches until I explained to them the 'why'.

Writing this book made me consider my 'why' in church marketing more than ever. Writing this book has not been easy. Why did I find it so important to write a book filled with church marketing advice? Because I have a deep passion to help others like you, who are in the same positions I have found myself in.

Yes, as church marketers, we write social media posts, we design graphics, we create a guest connection card, we make church bulletins, and the list goes on, but we serve a greater purpose than that. So, again, I ask why do you do what you do? Why do you share?

Exercise: Write down your personal 'why'. Really delve into the reasons that you are doing this work. Look back on this when you find yourself feeling overwhelmed and then remember the ultimate 'why' behind your work, because it is what you are called to do.

Ultimately, as a Christian, we share because we are commanded to. To go and share is explicitly said by Jesus Himself in the Great

Commission. Sharing is literally our mission. In each of the four Gospels, Matthew, Mark, Luke, and John all give accounts of Jesus giving this commission instruction that we as Christians take today as our overarching purpose statement. Here is the Great Commission in each of the four Gospels:

> *Matthew 28:19-20: "Therefore go and make disciples of all nations, baptizing them in the name of the Father and of the Son and of the Holy Spirit, and teaching them to obey everything I have commanded you. And surely I am with you always, to the very end of the age." (NIV)*

In Matthew's account, the most famous account of the Great Commission, we are charged to go and make disciples in all nations, baptize them, and teach them to obey Jesus.

> *Mark 16:15: "He said to them, 'Go into all the world and preach the gospel to all creation.'" (NIV)*

In Mark's account, Jesus tells His disciples to go into the world and preach the Gospel to everyone.

> *Luke 24:46-47: "He told them, 'This is what is written: The Messiah will suffer and rise from the dead on the third day, and repentance for the forgiveness of sins will be preached in his name to all nations, beginning at Jerusalem.'" (NIV)*

In Luke's account, Jesus tells His disciples that the Gospel should be preached to the entire world.

> *John 20:21: "Again Jesus said, 'Peace be with you! As the Father has sent me, I am sending you.'" (NIV)*

In John's account, John keeps it simple in his account of Jesus' words to His disciples regarding what they are to do. Just as God sent Jesus,

Jesus is sending us to declare His name and the Good News.

With all four accounts, Jesus tells His disciples to go and share the Gospel with the people across the entire world. That is an active statement. Go is a verb. Go is an action. Share is a verb. It is an action.

Jesus is sending us on purpose, with a purpose, and for a purpose. That purpose is to share His name and the redemption story to people in all nations. That is our 'why'. That is what motivates us. That is why we share, because we are commanded and sent by the King of the Kings, the Savior of the world.

So if you are ever feeling discouraged in this church marketing role you find yourself in and feel like just giving up, remember this: *God has called you to be His messenger to share the Good News with a lost a dying world, and He is sending you on purpose, with a purpose, and for a purpose.*

We often refer to the Gospel as Good News because it is just that, Good News. I love what my pastor has said before, "It's not Good News if no one shares it." This is so true. If we, as Christians, don't share the Gospel, who will? If we, as churches, don't share the Gospel, who will? How can we expect a lost and dying world to come to know Jesus if no one is willing to share Jesus with them?

As people working in ministry, I have to assume that you have been saved and that you know Jesus. But I want you to think back to when someone first shared Jesus with you. Maybe it was your parents, grandparents, a friend, a Sunday School teacher that shared Jesus with you the first time. Whoever it was and wherever it happened, someone saw it important enough to share Jesus with you. What if that person had not shared Jesus with you? Would you know Him today? Or would you be in the lost crowd of the world aimlessly wandering through life?

In the same way that someone saw it important enough to share Jesus with you, we should find it crucial to share Jesus with others. There are people in this world depending on you to share Jesus with them for the first time. Do not miss out on the opportunities to share Jesus with others.

I was recently sitting in a student conference where the guest speaker's sermon was focused on what our purpose is. I love messages like this because, again, we are people that are constantly searching for answers about our purpose in life. As I sat in a balcony and looked overhead at the gathering of over three hundred middle and high school students, I literally watched students sit up a little straighter when the speaker made the topic of his sermon known. I smiled at this because I thought to myself, "There are students searching for answers, searching for meaning, searching for their purpose, searching for their 'why'. Some of them think they are about to get their life plan exactly laid out for them out for them right here and now."

As the guest speaker preached his message, I loved how simply he broke down our purpose as Christians: "To know God and to make God known." Our purpose is two-fold: (1) to know God and (2) make God known. So, once we know God, we don't stop there and sit back twiddling our thumbs. We are to go and make God known. That is our purpose. That is our why. We share because we want and are commanded to make God known.

Again, if we don't make God known, who will? If churches are not proactive in sharing the name of Jesus and the Gospel, then who will? In the Sermon on the Mount, Jesus shared to those that listened to Him that:

"You are the salt of the earth. But if the salt loses its saltiness, how can it be made salty again? It is no longer good for anything, except to be thrown out and trampled underfoot. You are the light of the world. A town built on a hill cannot be hidden. Neither do people light a lamp and put it under a bowl. Instead they put it on its stand, and it gives light to everyone in the house. In the same way, let your light shine before others, that they may see your good deeds and glorify your Father in heaven." - Matthew 5:13-16 (NIV)

One of my family's dearest friends was a great leader in our community, local school system, and the church I was raised in. Godly wisdom and leadership literally exuded out of this woman. One of her greatest sayings that I ever heard her say was, "Salt does not do you any good if you keep inside the saltshaker."

Salt has a profound purpose. It is a well-known food preservative and food flavoring agent. There are specific and obvious reasons we use salt. For centuries, people have used salt to preserve foods, such as meats, to keep them from going bad, and salt continues to be one of the most commonly used flavoring agents to make food taste better. If salt is not salty, then it has no purpose. If salt is not poured out on food to either preserve or flavor it, then it serves no purpose either.

Without salt added to preserve it, what once seemed like perfectly good food to consume goes bad and perishes. Without salt added to flavor it, what looks like perfectly good food to consume is actually bland and without flavor. It needs salt to bring out and accentuate the food's natural flavors.

The same goes for us as humans. Without any type of added preservative, we are a deteriorating and dying species. Our flesh, though while it may look well, will eventually perish unless there is an added preservative. The only preservative we have is Jesus. We literally need Jesus (the salt) added to us and covering us for us to be preserved for eternity. Our flesh may look perfectly good on the outside and we are tempted to call ourselves good people, but when you actually get to know us, we are bland and without flavor. I mean we are a sinful and dying flesh; there is no way that tastes good. We need a flavoring agent to add flavor and to accentuate what God originally created when He created each of us. If Jesus is not poured out on us, then we have no flavor and we are dying. When churches have been given a saltshaker, we have been called to shake it out and spread it, not to keep it in.

As Jesus continued in His sermon, He tells that people do not light a lamp only to put it under a bowl. People light a lamp to give off light and to light a way. People light a lamp and put it on a stand so that it gives off light in the greatest way possible. As Christians, we have the opportunity to light the path that guides people to the Way, the Truth, and the Life. That is not something to be kept shaded or under a bowl. That is something to be lit and put on a lamp stand so that as many people as possible can see the ultimate source of light, Jesus.

Ultimately, we spread the salt across the world, and we light the way for the world not for our own personal glory or our local church's glory, but for God's glory. Why we share is not about us as individuals or us as a local church, we share for Him and on His behalf. The Church is His House, not ours. In Paul's letter to the Church of Corinth, he writes to the Corinthians that, "We are therefore Christ's ambassadors, as though God were making his appeal through us" (2 Corinthians 5:20, NIV).

We are Christ's representatives. When He ascended back to heaven forty days after His resurrection, He entrusted us to continue His ministry here on Earth until His return. While we do not possess and have the salvation power, we have the power of sharing and planting seeds. We are His representatives. God is using us as vessels to speak and work through us, making His appeal through us to the surrounding lost and dying world.

Church marketer or not, this title of Christ's ambassadors is given to all Christians. If we have been given the title of Christ's ambassadors, what are we doing with it? As a church marketer though, we have an even greater responsibility and task ahead of us to ensure we are sharing our local church's story and the message of the cross.

You may be saying though, "Madisen, you don't understand. My church is not that big. It does not matter if I share or not. My platform is not that big. My church's platform is not that big. What's the point?"

Simple. Do it for the one.

Why you share is for the one. Do it for the one. Again, as we discussed in the audience chapter about who's your one. One local church cannot reach every person in the world. However, if we all divide and conquer, then our reach is limitless. One person may be waiting on you. One person may be waiting on your church. Jesus is waiting on you to share. He wants to use you, but you have to let Him. Share for the one that needs Jesus.

In the marketing world, marketers have to become good at figuring out what people need and want before people even realize what they need and want. One of the best visionaries who was able to identify and tell consumers what they needed and wanted before they realized they needed and wanted it was Steve Jobs. Honestly, without Steve Jobs, would we have known that we needed personal computers, an electronic music player we could download music to and fit in our pocket, or that we needed a super phone that was actually a mighty computer that could fit in our pockets? No, yet our lives cannot simply function in society today without these products.

People who don't know Jesus don't know they need Jesus. Paul writes to the Corinthians that "the message of the cross is foolishness to those who are perishing, but to us who are being saved it is the power of God" (1 Corinthians 1:18, NIV). To everyone that we share Jesus with, we will not experience a 100% reception rate.

There will be mocking, laughing, anger, and even straight up being ignored. We share Jesus and invite people to church because they don't know they need Jesus. Lost people need advocates who will share Jesus with them. Lost people need churches who will actively pursue them and share with them about Jesus. They are perishing and do not even know it. For those of us who are saved though, the message of the cross is the power of God and we have a commandment and a purpose to go and share that message of the cross equipped by God's power.

Why we share as Christians and church marketers should not only be to gain something in return and reward. However, there is a great reward to be had when we work toward fulfilling our purpose to make God known.

In the recent student conference I mentioned where the guest speaker talked about our purpose as Christians, this conference was one that I had the opportunity and honor to be a part of the planning team for. Our church and team had done months of planning for this one event and during the week of the event it was a madhouse in the final preparations. We had to be reminded of our 'why' often to keep us motivated and going. This student conference was a huge event in our area where student ministries from over twenty churches in our area came together for one weekend, totaling nearly 2,000 total people including middle and high school students, student pastors, small group leaders, and more.

Over the years, I have had the opportunity to be a student at this event during my middle and high school years, be a small group leader, and then be a part of the planning team for a second host location that had to be opened up due to event growth. Starting as a student in the first year of this event leading to being a part of one location's planning team was a huge full circle moment for me and will forever be a highlight of my career and my ministry. Like I said though, in those final days leading to the event and even during the actual event, it was a literal madhouse. Just on my end, there was social media to be handled, a merchandise table with apparel, photography, visual production, photo booths, and bumper videos. Everyone else on our planning team was running around too with endless tasks to accomplish. We had other churches coming on our campus, we had guest speakers, a guest band, volunteers, this was our first year hosting the event, and more importantly we had students sitting in our seats that had never heard the name of Jesus before.

The evening before the first night of the event, I was preparing and emailing spending reports for marketing this event to one pastor and his email reply made me pause in the moment to just remember my 'why' and to thank God for allowing me to do what He has called me to do. His reply: *"May the reward for your labor be a harvest of souls! Salvation is priceless."*

During the final session of the conference, the guest speaker led into an invitation where he asked students to stand up in front of hundreds of others if they were lost and needed to be saved. In a room full of hundreds of teenagers, it got awkwardly silent really quick with this call-to-action, but then one student boldly stood up. Then there was another and then another one and then by the end the altar was full. We literally witnessed and saw a harvest of souls come to know the

Lord that night. A priceless moment.

Hearing students declare the name of Jesus as they boldly worshiped that night to end the event was a priceless moment. Seeing friends embrace each other at the end of the night as they left our campus. A priceless moment. Every late night. Every frustration. Every word typed on social networks. Every t-shirt folded. Every lanyard clipped to a volunteer name tag. It was all worth it.

Hearing the stories even after the event and witnessing the revival that happened in the lives of the students that attended was priceless. Church marketing and ministry as a whole is not for the weary. It does not come with fame and not always with the greatest budgets or monetary rewards. However, you cannot put a price tag on what we get to do and why we get to do it.

Yes, it's important to know your church's 'who, what, where, when, and how', but it means nothing if you do not know and forget your church's 'why'. On a personal note, it's also important to know who you are, what you do, where/when you are called to do it, and how to do it, but it means nothing if you do not know or forget your personal 'why'. As a church marketer and being in ministry, you will face opposition, frustrations, and hardships, but remember why you do what you do.

When you remember why you do what you do, may it compel you to go out and share like never before. When you do, may your reward for your labor be the greatest reward there is available, a harvest of souls. May your reward be filled with people coming to know Jesus, and then may they be compelled to go and share the name of Jesus with others. This has exponential potential, but it starts with you and me. Sharing your church's story, sharing the gospel message, and inspiring others in your church to share as well. Remember why you share. Don't let being overwhelmed as a church marketer stop you from sharing what He has called you to. He promises that His peace, a peace that surpasses all senses of fear and being overwhelmed, is with you. He is sending you, so don't be silent. Go and share. It's your purpose. It's your 'why'.

CHAPTER 11
NOW WHAT?

I cannot believe we have made it to the end, but I am reminded that this is only the beginning for both of us. This book is but a launching pad. This book was meant to provide a framework for you to take and apply to your own church marketing plan. As much as this book was meant to provide you answers, it was meant to spark more questions for you as well.

So now that you have reached this last chapter, you may be asking, "Now what?" That two worded question can bring excitement but also may bring back those feelings of being overwhelmed because it just seems like more work.

To answer the question of "now what", the first step is review everything that we went over throughout this book. Does your church know the 'who', 'what', 'where/when', and 'why'? Then once you've answered those questions, do you know 'how' to accomplish it? If not, start answering these questions. Sit down with your pastor and other church leaders to answer these questions.

Knowing these answers not only will help you as a church marketer, but they will also help you as a church overall. It is like putting a puzzle together. When all the puzzle pieces are in the box and not put together, the picture it is attempting to showcase may not make sense. Once you start putting the pieces together though, the picture comes to life and it all makes sense.

These six questions are meant to be puzzle pieces for your church and church marketing. They may not make sense or seem of much importance by themselves, but when you put the pieces (questions) together, it all showcases the picture of your church. So, start putting the puzzle together.

The second step in this "now what" is to determine what you need to learn. What do you need to absolutely learn right now and what do you need to work toward learning in the future? If there are platforms that your church will be present on now after reading this book, then learn those platforms.

Whatever you need to learn to get the job done, learn it. We are living in a time where the learning resources we have available at our disposal are limitless. With many being relatively low cost and even free sometimes, it is not too late for you to learn.

In fact, we must constantly keep learning. You may have graduated from high school or college, but you never graduate from being a student. You must constantly keep learning because the minute you stop learning is the moment you quit growing. Learning yields growth.

Growth is imperative for marketing because platforms and equipment are always evolving in order to reach people. Remember, your 'how' will change.

The thought of learning may overwhelm you though because you don't know where to start. Reach out to me. I am here to help you. I am here to help you learn. I didn't just write this book to feed you fish. I wrote this book to teach you how to fish. It's like the proverb says, "Feed a man a fish, you feed him for a day. Teach a man to fish and you feed him for a lifetime."

I want to teach you how to fish because church marketing is a fishing job, not just a well-prepared fish platter at your favorite seafood restaurant.

The third step is to take this six-question framework to apply to your own church projects. It will make gathering information for your church events and projects easier. It takes the guessing out of when the student ministry is having a camp and where it will be, for example, because you made sure from the beginning that you answered all the pertinent questions to gather the necessary info.

The fourth step is to trust your calling and trust God who gave you that calling. Why? Because God is in control and He gave you your calling for a purpose. God has given specific gifts, talents, abilities, and platforms to you and your church.

These specifics that He has given you may look completely different than the next church marketer and church. Remember though, don't fall into the comparison trap that sends you into the tailspin of a pity party and paralyzes you in your tracks to not do anything.

At the same time, don't let what God has gifted you and your church make you prideful either. Because these gifts, talents, abilities, and platforms do not belong to you anyway. They belong to God.

While these specifics He has given you and your church may look different than the next church marketer and church, your

responsibility as a church marketer remains the same.
As a church marketer, you must remember that your ultimate responsibility is to remain faithful and use your God given talents, abilities, and gifts for the advancement of His Kingdom. As a church, your church must remember the ultimate responsibility is to remain faithful and use their God given talents, abilities, and gifts for the advancement of His Kingdom.

God gave these to you for a specific reason. That reason is to bring people to salvation. To use these for the advancement of His Kingdom and His glory.

When you are feeling overwhelmed, it can cause you to feel unsure of this calling. Trust me. I've been there. In the moments of being overly overwhelmed or frustrated, I've told God, "There's no way this is what you have called me to." In the moments of feeling overwhelmed and frustrated, I've even asked God, "Why did you call me into this?"

Even in those moments, you must remember your calling and trust your calling. Even in those moments, you must remember who God is and that He knew what He was doing when He gave you this calling. He knows where you've been, where you are, and where you're going.

There's comfort in that. There's comfort in remembering that God knows where we are headed.

When Moses was telling the Israelites that he would not be crossing the Jordan into the Promised Land with them, he told them that it would be Joshua that would lead them. To the Israelites, Moses spoke these powerful words of encouragement to them, "Be strong and courageous. Do not be afraid or terrified because of them, for the Lord your God goes with you; he will never leave you nor forsake you" (Deuteronomy 31:6, NIV).

On a more individual note, Moses turned to Joshua to give him words of encouragement in front of the Israelites. It mirrored much of what he told the Israelites but this was one-on-one encouragement. Moses reiterated to Joshua, "The Lord himself goes before you and will be with you; he will never leave you nor forsake you. Do not be afraid; do not be discouraged" (Deuteronomy 31:8, NIV).

While I'm in no way comparing myself to Moses, I do think of our relationship that we've built over this book to be similar to a Moses and Joshua type relationship. I can lead you up until this point of church marketing, but now it is your turn to lead in your church. It's time for you to lead in your church marketing.

So, to your church as a whole and in the words of Moses, I encourage your church to be strong and courageous because God goes with you and He will never leave nor forsake you.

To you as a church leader and church marketer, I encourage you to not be afraid nor be discouraged because God will not leave you nor forsake you. He has already gone before you and will be with you as you go.

In your calling, God will not lead you where He has not already been and is not willing to go with you Himself.

If He has gone before you and promises to go with you, then trust Him. Trust His calling on your life no matter how difficult it is and how overwhelming and frustrating it can get sometimes.

God knows what He has called you to and where He is leading you. Therefore, He promises to equip you in your calling to be prepared for who and where He is calling you to.

I love how the writer of Hebrews reminds us of God's promise to equip us. The writer of Hebrews reminds us that God will "equip you with everything good for doing his will, and may he work in us what is pleasing to him, through Jesus Christ, to whom be glory for ever and ever. Amen" (Hebrews 13:21, NIV).

While you may not have the answer every time and while your marketing plans may even fail, trust Him and leave the rest to Him. When it is out of your control, leave it to the One who has all things under His control.

Does that mean you throw out all your marketing plans, what you've read in this book, and what you've learned? No. Leaving it to God does not mean you sit on the 'seat of doing nothing' while becoming a master thumb twiddler.

It means you are trusting Him, His calling for you, and surrendering to Him with a heart of obedience.

In Paul's letter to the Romans, Paul reminds them that, "everyone who calls on the name of the Lord will be saved" (romans 10:13, NIV). However, he continues on to ask: How anyone can call on the name of the Lord if they do not know the name of the Lord? Paul puts it like this, "How can they believe in the one of whom they have not heard? And how can they hear without someone preaching to them?" (Romans 10:14, NIV).

If people need to be preached to in order to learn and know about God to ultimately call upon His name to be saved, then how can we preach to them? Paul puts it like this, "And how can anyone preach unless they are sent?" (Romans 10:15, NIV).

As a church marketer, you may or may not be a pastor, but make no mistake that you have been sent. Sent to share God and the Gospel. If you have been saved and are a Christian, you have been sent.

Those that are sent are the hands and feet of Jesus. You are the hands and feet of Jesus. As Paul reminds the Romans, "how beautiful are the feet of those who bring good news." (Romans 10:15, NIV).

Sharing the Good News is not always easy. Church marketing is not always easy. Your shoes may get holes in them as you keep walking. Your socks may become threadbare. Your feet may get blisters, calluses, or cuts. No matter how difficult it may look or how bad your feet may look with all the walking you are doing to share the Good News, God considers your feet to be beautiful for sharing the Good News.

As a church marketer, what you do now will reach someone that has never heard the Gospel. As a church marketer, what you do now is Kingdom work and has Kingdom impact.

Don't forget this framework of these six essential marketing questions. Ask yourself these questions as a Christian. Ask yourself these questions as a church marketer. Ask your church leadership these questions. More importantly, seek God for the answers to these questions. Don't forget to seek Him in all that you do.

Who has God called your church to be? Who has God called you to reach? What has God called you to share? Where has He called you to share? When has He called you to share? How has God called you to share it? All the answers to those questions point back to your purpose. They point back to why God has called you.

Church marketer, I want to help you. Church marketer, I want to teach you. Church marketer, I am with you on this journey. That's why I wrote this book.

As difficult as writing this book may have been at times, God is the one that gave me the knowledge, wisdom, words, and strength to write and finish this book. I know there is a specific reason and a specific person that I wrote this book for. I believe that person is you. Yes, you. Don't look over your shoulder looking for someone else.

I wrote this book for you because I believe you are searching for answers right now. You don't know where to start in church marketing. Or maybe you have found yourself stagnant. Or maybe you want to learn more, be more, and do more in this marketing field, the church, and the world for His name's sake.

When church marketing feels overwhelming, remember the stained-glass window icon on the cover of this book. Remember your church's who, what, when, where, why, and how. Keep your window clean and clear to allow you and your church to see the lost and dying world on the outside that's waiting to hear a life-changing message and also allow the world to see the beauty found inside the church. Lastly, keep the cross in the center of it all. This is what makes church marketing simple.

Church marketer, I'm praying for you. That's how we will end this book, with a prayer.

God, I thank you for who You are. Thank You for what You have done, are doing, and will continue to do. God, I thank You that Your promises are always yes and amen despite how uncertain and dark our world may seem at times.

I thank you for this reader. I thank you for creating them. I thank you for creating them on purpose and for a purpose. I thank you for saving them. I thank you for calling them into this ministry. I thank you for the specific abilities, gifts, platforms, and talents you have given this reader. Thank you for the story You have given them. I thank you for going before them and continuing to be with them every step of the way.

God, remind them right now who they are and who they belong to, You. Remind them right now that You are with them and for them.

God, if this reader is feeling overwhelmed, anxious, nervous, or paralyzed in this church marketing world or whatever aspect of life may have them feeling like they are stuck in quicksand, may You make Your presence clear and evident to them right now. God, let this reader feel your love, peace, and comfort like never before.

Give this reader the knowledge, the wisdom, and the ability to learn to accomplish Your plans and Your purpose. God, equip them like You promise to do to live out the calling You have placed on their life.

God, may they feel confident in their equipment. May they seek You in all things.

God, I pray for the church this reader is a part of. May You shower this church with Your blessings. God, may You multiply their disciples, and may You multiply their reach.

May this church know who they are, who they are to reach, what they are sharing, where and when they are to share it, and how they are specifically supposed to share and reach. May they not be distracted and pursue You and their specific mission and purpose You have called them to.

God, thank You for being in control of all things. May this reader and their church not dwell on the things they cannot control but may they surrender it all to you. May they feel You lift the burden of the uncontrollable and focus on You.

God, may the world see You and know You through this church marketer and their church.

Let us decrease so that You may increase. Let Your shine brighter through us that people of this world have no doubt that it is not us but You.

Though troubles, hardships, and obstacles will come, God thank You for continuing to give us strength to continue to push forward.

May we go where You call us to go no matter how unchartered the waters may seem. May we live a life of obedience in all that we do.

God, I pray for this reader. Bless their ministry. Bless their family. Bless them as an individual. Give them answers, God, as they seek Your face. Give them strength. Give them comfort. Give them peace. Give them knowledge. Give them the resources they need to accomplish Your will.

God, You are the author of all things, so I thank You for these words You have given me to write in this book. May You use these words to somehow speak to this reader for a specific reason. God, use this book to multiply and advance Your Kingdom.

God, use this church marketer and their church to multiply and advance Your Kingdom. As Paul writes, since You are for us, God, who can be against us? Thank you for this promise.

Let us remember this and allow it to motivate us. God, we love You and we thank You. May our tongues continuously repeat, "To Him who sits on the throne and to the Lamb be praise and honor and glory and power, for ever and ever" (Revelation 5:13, NIV). No matter what, we will give you all the honor, glory, and praise for it all.

It is in Your name that I humbly pray. Amen.

ACKNOWLEDGEMENTS

While my name may be on the cover of this book, there are numerous people that have stood behind through the years to support me. Without their love and support, I would not be where I am today nor would even the thought of writing a book have been possible. To name everyone would be to write an entirely additional book, and even then there would still be people that I would leave out. However, before I get to the specific names and people that I would like to acknowledge for my first book, let me give one big shout out to my family and friends. Thank you is not adequate to express my gratitude to each of you. God has blessed me tremendously with what I consider the best family and friends that anyone could have.

To the readers, thank you for reading this book. Thank you for giving me a chance! You will always be a special group because you were the readers of my first book. God had you in mind before I even had the outline of this book finished.

To my parents, Marlon and Kris (or Daddy and Mama as I call them), most people's failures are a result of a lack of parental support. That has never been the case with you both as my parents. For someone as undeserving as me, I do not know what I did for God to bless me with two of the most Godly parents that a daughter could ever have. Your support and love for me has always been above and beyond what anyone could ask for. When I said, "I am going to write a book," your answers were, "What's the first one going to be about?" I could go on and on about how thankful I am for both of you. Thank you for both your sacrifices through the years to ensure that I always had the best education and resources to achieve my dreams. Thank you for always pushing me to chase God's dreams for me even when I didn't think it was possible! I love you and I thank you. One of life's greatest blessings is to be called your daughter.

To my brother, Chandler, you are not only one of the most Godly people that I know but you are one of the wisest people that I know despite you being almost four years younger than me. I thank God that He not only gave me a brother but that He gave me a built-in best friend with you and the ultimate Disney-ride partner! Thank you for listening to my rants and calmly replying with the most sound advice always. When I was questioning what to do with my next steps, you always were the one saying, "I think you need to start by writing a book and then I think everything will become clearer." You were right! Thank you for being the first person to ever read this book! Thank you for letting me pick your brain after you were done reading! Chandler, I cannot wait to see what God has in store for you. Your future is bright! Your gifts and abilities are unparalleled. Thank you for being you! Thank you for being my brother!

Failing to mention schools in this would erase part of my story where I got my start.

To the teachers of Jones Elementary, thank you for helping lay the foundation. While this gem of a school may be a completely different school now, the foundation that these teachers laid here for me will not be forgotten. You were the ones who always encouraged my writing no matter how bad those creative writing stories I would write were.

To the Da Vinci Academy, for some reason, you saw potential in me before I even became a teenager and you pushed me towards that potential. To Gary Martin, I say thank you for throwing that Adobe CS4 Photoshop book at me that day in class. That started it all.

To Chestatee High School, thank you for every opportunity that you gave me! For every sign and banner printed and to every logo designed. For everything! The administration and teachers that allowed me to pave my own way in high school even when there were not actual graphic design classes, I say thank you for your support. There are too many teachers to name and thank. Trust me though, I will find some way to show my appreciation to you directly through this book. However, I have to say thank you to Nick Scheman for giving that girl with the t-shirt design on her iPad a chance. You daring to chase the impossible in education allowed me to have some of the best teachers and opportunities a person could ever ask for. It paved the way for so many opportunities inside and outside of those walls for so many including me! To the Honors Mentorship Program, thank you for providing students with internship opportunities to start pursuing their dreams beyond the four walls of the classroom! Go War Eagles!

To Liberty University, for all those late nights, long papers, and making me learn how to love lots of coffee, I say thank you for the educational opportunities you provided me to earn both my undergraduate and graduate degrees. As a Champion of Christ, I hope to take what you taught me and change the world one person at a time.

To Self Publishing School, I say thank you for forcing me to get it in gear and to actually write this book! None of this would have ever been achieved without you. To Chandler and your team, I say thank you for what you do to help make aspiring authors' dreams like mine come to fruition. To Sloane, I say thank you for being my coach through this entire process! Thank you for continuing to push me even when I felt like giving up. I am so thankful for you! To my editor, Hannah, you helped me transform this book into something that I did not think it could be. Thank you for handling my book with such care every step of the way.

To the churches, there are three churches that I must mention. The first is Mountain View Baptist Church, the church where I was born and raised. To Mountain View, I say thank you. Thank you for being the source of so many good memories. Thank you for even inspiring the cover of this book. I struggled with how to design the cover and when I closed my eyes to think about church in relation to this book cover all I saw was the stained glass windows inside the sanctuary. It brought the flood of memories and I knew that these beautiful stained glass windows also showed the beauty of church marketing. Thank you for helping my parents lay the spiritual foundation for me. Thank you for teaching me about Jesus and showing me the love of Christ. Thank you for beginning the discipleship process. This is the place where I began my relationship with Christ. This is where I was baptized. This is where I was raised. This is one of my homes. I often ask God why He called me away from here but I understand that if I never stepped out I never would have lived through so many of the opportunities God has provided me with. The heritage in this small church in the fork of the road is rich, and I'm so thankful that God planted my roots here.

To Pleasant Hill Baptist Church, you were the church where I spent my teenage years. This was the church where I first heard God say,

"What are you doing for me?" This is where I learned what ministry was and what it involved. This was the first church where I interned. In this place, God placed in my path incredible people that left a lasting impact on my life. To all those people, including my amazing youth leaders, I say thank you!

To Chestnut Mountain Church, I do not know where to begin because I owe this book to you. You are the source of inspiration for this. You are featured in just about every story in this book actually. I say thank you for taking that 16 year old girl in and giving her the opportunity of a lifetime. Thank you for allowing me to come back and be the Director of Marketing and Communications! This church is special and I'm blessed to call it home. To the pastors and staff of this church, while the people on the team have changed over the years, it has been one of my greatest honors to serve alongside each of you. You didn't let my youth despise me but instead encouraged and pushed me to use the talents and abilities God has given me! I love you, Chestnut Mountain Church, and I'm so thankful that God has granted me the gift of sharing your story and being a voice for you over the years. Thank you to my interns over the past two years who showed me how powerful it is to empower others in church marketing. It is inspiring to see how God is continuing to use you all and grow you in the creative fields that you are all in. Thank you for teaching me even when I was supposed to be teaching you. Thank you for making me fall in love with church marketing and church communications. To the current CMC team, Brian, Jared, Brandon, Brandon, Tim, Angie, June, Sam, Ingrid, Sam, and Chase, I say thank you to each of you! You inspire me daily and I am so thankful to call you ministry partners and friends!

To the most important One, I say thank you to God. You are the Source! The source of life, the source of salvation, the source of creation, the source of purpose. Thank you for everything that You have given to me even though I am so unworthy. Thank you for calling me! Thank you for the gifts and abilities You have given me. Thank you for giving me the words, knowledge, opportunity, strength, and stamina to write this book. God, I owe it all to you! Lord, I love You. May You receive all the honor, glory, and praise for this all!

DON'T FORGET YOUR FREE GIFT!

**Thanks for reading this book!
Don't forget to download your free guide!**

**DOWNLOAD THIS GUIDE FOR FREE NOW:
www.madisenmayfield.com/mcms**

LET ME KNOW WHAT YOU THINK!

**I appreciate your feedback and ask that you
please leave a review on Amazon to let me and
other future readers know what you thought of this book!**

Thank you so much!

- Madisen Mayfield

ABOUT THE AUTHOR

Madisen Mayfield is a Georgia native. Madisen says that the starting point for her love of branding, graphic design, marketing, and communications began in middle school when she began learning Adobe Photoshop. Throughout high school, Madisen continued to build her skills through education learned in the classroom, by herself, and through numerous opportunities provided to her by her teachers and others in the community. With strong conviction, Madisen entered the church marketing world in her junior year of high school as a graphic design intern. For the remainder of high school and during her undergraduate studies in college, Madisen continued building her skillset as an intern, freelancer, and volunteer for churches, non-profit organizations, and small businesses of all sizes. In obtaining her Bachelor of Science in Business Administration: Digital Marketing and Advertising and her Master of Arts in Strategic Communication from Liberty University along with her extensive experience, Madisen is an emerging leader in the industry carving herself to be an expert branding, communications, creative, and marketing specialist. Madisen is passionate about guiding organizations and people to discover and share their identity, their audience, their message, and their purpose.

Follow and connect with Madisen to learn more tips and how you can both work together.

madisenmayfield.com
hello@madisenmayfield.com
Follow Madisen on Facebook, Instagram, and Twitter: @madisenmayfield

Made in the USA
Columbia, SC
01 September 2022

65589577R00080